DEAD CAT BOUNCE

BY MARY RACHEL BROWN

CURRENCY PRESS
The performing arts publisher

GRIFFIN THEATRE COMPANY

CURRENT THEATRE SERIES

First published in 2019
by Currency Press Pty Ltd,
PO Box 2287, Strawberry Hills, NSW, 2012, Australia
enquiries@currency.com.au
www.currency.com.au

in association with Griffin Theatre Company

Typeset by Dean Nottle for Currency Press.
Cover shows Kate Cheel.
Cover photo by Brett Boardman. Cover design by Alphabet.

Currency Press acknowledges the Traditional Owners of the Country on which
we live and work. We pay our respects to all Aboriginal and Torres Strait
Islander Elders, past and present.

A catalogue record for this
book is available from the
NATIONAL LIBRARY National Library of Australia
OF AUSTRALIA

Contents

For Maria.

Dead Cat Bounce was first produced by Griffin Theatre Company at SBW Stables Theatre, Sydney, on 22 February 2019, with the following cast:

MATILDA	Kate Cheel
ANGELA	Lucia Mastrantone
TONY	Johnny Nasser
GABE	Josh Quong Tart

Director, Mitchell Butel
Designer, Genevieve Blanchett
Lighting Designer, Alexander Berlage
Composer and Sound Designer, Nate Edmondson
Stage Manager, Michelle Sverdlorff
Stage Management Secondment, Jennifer Jackson

CHARACTERS

GABRIEL FREEMAN, 48
ANGELA MORETTI, 44
MATILDA BLACKWELL, 24
TONY BEST, 42

NOTE

I encourage the producer to collaborate with artists from diverse backgrounds in the realisation of this work and to consider gender equity in the engagement of all creatives.

MRB

This play went to press before the end of rehearsals and may differ from the play as performed.

SCENE ONE—THE LAST MAN STANDING

GABRIEL: I cleaned the house, showered, shaved, ironed, dressed. Dressed for success. Even my socks were matching. I clocked myself in the mirror and raised my glass. 'You deserve this.'

Beat.

I closed the door and the window, sat down, chose a spot on the wall, lined my life up and aimed. Every mistake, every lie, regret, doubt, deceit, delete, delete, delete. Disgust is a great motivator, by the end of the bottle I'd murdered every inch of the room, except the slow drip, drip of the tap. I eyeballed the sink, I didn't need reminding of what it means to be alone.

Beat.

I should've googled it, worked out what I was in for. Gas hurts, it burns, the eyes, ears, nose, throat and lungs, then it rises before finishing the job. I turned my gaze to the ceiling.

Beat.

Jesus.

Pause.

I'd left the skylight open.

I lit a cigarette before turning the oven off. The bar lowers a bit when you've failed at killing yourself. I couldn't inhale, but it was a comfort, the back and forth of smoking. And just as I was settling back into the rhythmic imitation of life—Bang! Out of nowhere, there was Angela.

'I need you to dig a hole.'

I was in no condition for digging, and Angela was in no condition for sympathy.

The most brutal evidence that you are alive is your ability to follow basic instructions. I did an excellent job, I went deep. She wanted to make sure that little fucker was dead and buried.

I tried to return the shovel, she wouldn't have a bar of it, Angela was done with me. Fair enough, I was done with me. Your mother was the last man standing. She took me to hospital and the floodgates opened.

There's a lot to do when you decide to live.

SCENE TWO—BEAUTIFUL PEOPLE

Gabriel's flat.

A couch and two bottles of wine, one empty.

MATILDA *is tapping her fingers in a way that mimics the sound of a horse's gallop.*

GABRIEL: Once upon a time—
MATILDA: When?
GABRIEL: The past.
MATILDA: That leaves it wide open?
GABRIEL: Fingers!

> MATILDA *stops tapping.*

Thank you. Once upon a time there was a cat.
MATILDA: I am a dog person—
GABRIEL: And this cat suffered from gigantism.
MATILDA: Gigantism?
GABRIEL: Type 'obese cats' into Google and you'll get fat fuckers everywhere.
MATILDA: So we got a big cat—
GABRIEL: That grew and grew and—
MATILDA: Grew, so what?
GABRIEL: If you were to fly from this cat's arsehole to its head it would take about a hundred hours.
MATILDA: With stops?
GABRIEL: Don't embroider.
MATILDA: You'd have to refuel.
GABRIEL: Just know, this cat ate in heaven and shat in hell. That's how big he was. He could destroy buildings with the twitch of his whiskers, cut holes in the ozone layer with the swagger of his tail. And when he moulted—
MATILDA: You're the embroiderer.
GABRIEL: One single hair could flatten a village.

MATILDA *starts tapping her fingers again.*

Every time he scratched, several million people died, and he was itchy by nature. Riddled with agitation. And fleas.

MATILDA: Filthy!

GABRIEL: Fingers!

MATILDA: Sorry!

She stops tapping her fingers.

GABRIEL: It's like a miniature pony, galloping all over my story flow.

MATILDA: Because I don't want some story you just pulled out of your arse, Gabe. I want the story you poured your heart and soul into.

GABRIEL: You can buy a copy when it is published, young lady.

MATILDA: I will, old man. I'll buy the hard copy and hit you over the head with it. Don't dangle me!

GABRIEL: You're adorable when you dangle.

MATILDA: Why won't you let me read it?

GABRIEL: Because I like you as you are, Matilda. Count yourself lucky I'm not one of those types that insists you read everything I write, and watches you do so, without blinking. A mouth breather, constantly asking you what page you're up to, and updating you on the status of my anxiety-induced diarrhoea whilst banging on about my crippling obsession with Hemingway.

MATILDA: You're not answering my question, Gabriel, why—

GABRIEL: People read my work and they change, they look at me differently.

MATILDA: I've read your work, and I don't—

GABRIEL: Everyone's read the first book. That's the problem. They look at me like they can see right through me now.

MATILDA: Do people ever read your work and look at you like this?

She attempts love eyes and fails.

No wait, this—no, this?

She clocks GABRIEL *with the look of love.*

Do they ever look at you with love?

Pause.

I can't hold it forever, Gabe.

GABRIEL: That's good ... because I feel like I am in a cult!

He catches her hurt.

A good cult!

Beat.

MATILDA: What does she see when she looks right through you?

GABRIEL: A market. It's work, Matilda, we meet, eat, drink, make small talk and I get my verdict.

MATILDA: From your ex-girlfriend publisher.

GABRIEL: Who I haven't seen for two years.

MATILDA: What about in your head? Have you seen her in your head?

GABRIEL: I haven't had anything in my head but work. I have been alone for two years.

MATILDA: Just you and your book, hey?

GABRIEL: Yep.

MATILDA: And now it's finished.

GABRIEL: Yep.

MATILDA: So you're free.

Beat.

Can you be free, Gabriel?

GABRIEL: I'm free ...

MATILDA: Invite her to dinner.

GABRIEL: Pardon?

MATILDA: Invite Anna to—

GABRIEL: Angela.

MATILDA: Whatever, invite her to dinner.

GABRIEL: For who? For you?

MATILDA: For all three of us.

Beat.

For freedom.

GABRIEL: Jesus ... Okay.

MATILDA: Good. We can discuss the book I haven't read.

GABRIEL: Adorable suits you better than jealous, Matilda.

MATILDA: Adorable makes me sound like a cartoon character!

GABRIEL: Do you actually know what adorable means?

MATILDA: I prefer what you called me last night.

GABRIEL: You're a double threat.

MATILDA: Let me read it—

GABRIEL: Triple threat. Sexy, adorable, and a little aggravating.

MATILDA: I am not adorable!

GABRIEL: Yes you are!

MATILDA: Shut up!

GABRIEL: Make me!

> MATILDA *kisses* GABRIEL *in a very non-adorable way.*

MATILDA: Told ya, not adorable. I win. Hand the book over.

GABRIEL: No.

MATILDA: Okay.

> *She gets up, ready to leave.*

No book, no cigar!

GABRIEL: Oh, come on? I don't want to look at what you do for work.

MATILDA: Data entry? You should try this 'cult' out one day, it's full of normal people—

GABRIEL: Normal?—

MATILDA: Normal, like me, that lay down their guns and risk showing what they feel.

GABRIEL: My book is not what I feel, it's what I do.

MATILDA: … If it's not about feeling, why do you write?

GABRIEL: Don't know how to do anything else.

MATILDA: I can get you a data entry job if you want?

GABRIEL: I'll keep that in mind.

MATILDA: Do you ever watch the news? I think you should lose the artistic angst, watch the news and get some perspective.

GABRIEL: Right.

MATILDA: A man got struck by lightning yesterday.

GABRIEL: Really?

MATILDA: Yep, at the love of his life's funeral, struck right in the heart and he dropped dead. In Kempsey Cemetery of all places.

GABRIEL: Well, people die every day, it's not really news, Matilda—

MATILDA: It was news! It was on the news! They said the lightning bolt struck at the exact time the first spade full of dirt hit the top of his wife's coffin. A lightning bolt!

GABRIEL: Don't watch TV.

MATILDA: No TV, no Facebook, no Twitter, no smart phone, no friends, no family—

GABRIEL: None that I would want to inflict upon you.

MATILDA: No car, no day job, no food in the fridge.

GABRIEL: There's wine.

MATILDA: Thank Christ you drink, otherwise I'd think you were just a figment of my imagination.

GABRIEL: I drink therefore I am.

MATILDA starts tapping.

Fingers!

MATILDA holds her hand.

MATILDA: Fine! I'll sit here, with my boyfriend, holding my own hand so I don't tap. Happy!

GABRIEL: What about using the power of your mind?

MATILDA: Doesn't work.

GABRIEL observes MATILDA holding her hand. He finds the performance endearing, She exploits his gaze.

Get me a drink.

GABRIEL refills her wine glass.

Don't get comfortable! When I can't tap other stuff makes its way to the surface.

GABRIEL: Does it?

MATILDA picks up the glass and drinks without unlocking her hands. Pause. She starts whistling. GABRIEL cuts her off.

Okay! Okay.

He removes the wine glass from her hands and holds her right hand.

Be patient with me, Matilda.

MATILDA: Don't ask for my patience if you're just entertaining yourself, Gabriel.

Beat.

GABRIEL: Without façade in contemporary society.

MATILDA: What?

GABRIEL: Adorable means without façade in contemporary society.

MATILDA: I bet she has façade. In contemporary society.

GABRIEL *lets go of* MATILDA*'s hand.*

GABRIEL: Jesus—

MATILDA *starts tapping her fingers.*

Fingers!

MATILDA: Fuck it!

She goes back to holding her hand again. GABRIEL *looks at her hands.*

Haven't you ever had a habit you didn't know about?

GABRIEL: How would I know?

MATILDA: Someone tells you. The one that really shocked me was my lips move when I read, I didn't know I was doing it until a group of school kids made fun of me on a bus. And I thought to myself, you have no fucking idea.

Beat.

I think the same about you sometimes. No idea. You'd let me read your book if you had any idea.

GABRIEL: Can we drop the book?

GABRIEL *pours himself a drink.*

MATILDA: Okay, I'll go and leave you two together.

GABRIEL: What?

MATILDA: You and your best friend, Artistic Angst.

GABRIEL: Very funny.

MATILDA: You can go fuck Artistic Angst's brains out for all I care.

GABRIEL: I might catch something.

MATILDA: You're the disease, Gabriel.

GABRIEL: I asked for your patience—

MATILDA: And I asked to read your book. You don't let me in, that's your bad habit.

GABRIEL: Okay, you want in, fine, little secret for you, I have no idea if the book is any good. I don't know what the publisher will say, what the public will say, what the critics will say, and what the bank will say if this doesn't work. Failure and success look very similar until you get up close and one of them slaps you in the face. You make fun of artistic angst but it has teeth when you're my age. You wake up one day and bang, you're fifty, fucked up and broke. You think it's funny I have no friends, and that I can't sit through dinner parties talking about mortgages, health insurance, designer dogs, white goods and the price of child care? And the other one, the hot topic—happiness! Jesus! It's exhausting enough without you on my back.

MATILDA: Sorry.

GABRIEL: Tap, tap tap, every time you don't get what you want! Life is not that simple. What is wrong with you? Why don't you think? Think!

> *Beat.* MATILDA *sits. She places her palms on her lap face up and looks at them.*

Sorry.

MATILDA: No, thank you. For filling in the gaps and giving me the chance not to get it wrong.

GABRIEL: You're not wrong … it's not wrong …

MATILDA: I know that. I don't think it's an accident when people like us stumble upon each other at an airport bar and then don't get out of bed for a week. Miss the world for a week, miss all those dinner-party conversations about white goods—

GABRIEL: You're too young to talk about white goods, Matilda.

MATILDA: And you're not boring enough to talk about them. It's no accident, it's called finding each other, Gabriel. And here's a little secret for you. My parents never read to me, never bought me a book. I read everything I thought I needed to know on Facebook. Then I went to art school and there were all these conversations I couldn't participate in. I used to study people like you, people I thought were smarter than me, and I'd copy them. Problem was, the people I wanted to know started to spot it. I know what it's like not to think. I didn't read a book till I was twenty-one, Gabriel.

GABRIEL: Twenty-one is long time to wait for the best friend you'll ever have. What about school? Didn't you have to read—?

MATILDA: No. I majored in cheating, smoking, drinking, benzos and sleeping with people, including my English teacher.

GABRIEL: What?

MATILDA: Amazing what you can do when you put your body to it. My art school teacher wasn't interested in me, weirdo.

GABRIEL: Lecturer.

Beat.

You slept—

MATILDA: I was looking for someone who could make me interesting. And he was looking for an escape from middle age. It was a mutual humiliation.

GABRIEL: Things are not mutual when you're—how old—?

MATILDA: Seventeen. It was only three times, and I got an A plus for Russian literature. So my parents were happy.

GABRIEL: Did your parents know?

MATILDA: No.

GABRIEL: Seventeen years old—

MATILDA: I am not asking for your sympathy or your value system. Don't need it. So drop it.

GABRIEL: Matilda—

MATILDA: Just know, I spent a lot of time off my face blaming gatekeepers for the fact that I didn't think I would amount to anything. I don't do that anymore. I walk right up to the gates and I say who I am, and what I want, I am here to know you. And besides the fact that I talk too much, there is nothing wrong with me, Gabriel.

Beat.

You can say something now.

Beat.

Say something!

GABRIEL: What was the first book you read?

MATILDA: I sat on a beach in the dead of summer reading about the dead of winter. While my friends were swimming, I was on the shore slaving away with the most miserable characters Russian literature had to offer. I wanted reading to be as hard as I thought it would be.

GABRIEL: *War and Peace?*

MATILDA: *Crime and Punishment.*

GABRIEL: Baptism by fire.

MATILDA: It was, until I got to the bit where the peasant beats the shit out of the donkey.

GABRIEL: It was a horse.

MATILDA: Same thing, service animal, he beat it to death, trying to make it perform. The book just read itself after that. All I had to do was turn pages. I have been making up for lost time ever since. So much so, I need glasses now. I wept like a baby when that donkey gave up and fell to its knees.

GABRIEL: It was a horse—

MATILDA: Donkey—horse! You're missing the point. Books trust you with inner worlds.

> *Beat.*

Good luck tomorrow. I genuinely hope she likes your book. I really do.

> MATILDA *gets up to leave.*

GABRIEL: Matilda!

> MATILDA *exits.*

… Christ.

> GABRIEL *finishes his wine. He opens another bottle, pours himself more wine. He puts a record on.*

> GABRIEL *lies down on the couch with his book,* For Whom the Bell Tolls. *He gets up and moves the bottle of wine closer to the couch. He briefly catches himself in the mirror. He resettles himself, just as he does* MATILDA *reappears, unnoticed by* GABRIEL. *She removes the needle from the record, creating an almighty scratching sound.*

Fuck!

> *Beat.* MATILDA *pours a large glass of wine and drinks a significant amount.*

MATILDA: I thought you were going to follow me. People usually follow me. You were supposed to follow me.

GABRIEL: Sorry, didn't know that was a rule.

> MATILDA *sits and looks at her upward-facing palms again.*

MATILDA: I know I am not meant to ask for a copy of your door key, boast about reading *Crime and Punishment*. Tell you I slept with my English teacher, be jealous of your ex, tell you my lips move when I read. Tell you you drink too much, and you should eat more, sleep more. I know I shouldn't clean your house, bring your mail in, take your garbage out, clean your jacket pockets out and try and pair up all your odd socks!

GABRIEL: What?

MATILDA: You need new socks.

> *Beat.*

I'll just keep walking round in the dark waiting for you to hurt me or love me. I can feel it.. I am even going to love you. I should hate. I am hardwired for it.

> *Pause.*

I think I scratched your record. Sorry.

GABRIEL: That's okay ... I think we should—why don't we start by—can we make a deal to stop scaring each other?

> MATILDA *is frozen.* GABRIEL *put his hand out. She takes his arm instead and pulls him close to her.*

MATILDA: Booh!

GABRIEL: Fuck!

MATILDA: I love you. Scares the crap out of you too, doesn't it?

> *Beat.*

GABRIEL: No.

MATILDA: Liar. 'Can we make a deal to stop scaring each other?' What's that? It sounds like some sort of shit you'd hear on daytime TV designed for half-alive people. I can't be a half-alive person for you, Gabe. I feel like I'm sitting on my hands.

GABRIEL: Well, you're not. You're tapping and waving them about. Come on, Matilda.

MATILDA: I should go. Don't worry, ignore everything I've said, I don't really love you with all my heart and fucking soul, I've just drunk too much, and I'm the kind of girl that cries at stories about people getting struck in the heart by lightning, so take no notice of me.

> *She gets up to go and yet again stops.*

One more thing, even if your book is shit, shit with steam coming off it, I am going to put a hard copy on my shelf. It is more than goose bumps. It's like I can feel all my internal organs. Even my hair hurts, that's how much I love you. Goodnight.

MATILDA *continues to exit but* GABRIEL *catches her.*

GABRIEL: Sit. And wait.

MATILDA: What—?

GABRIEL: And shut up.

> GABRIEL *exits.* MATILDA *sits. She start tapping her fingers and catches herself. She picks up the book that Gabriel was reading.*

MATILDA: *For Whom the Bell Tolls.* Bloody hell.

GABRIEL: [*offstage*] What?

MATILDA: Nothing.

> *She puts the book down and picks up the bottle of wine, looks at it and puts it down. She puts the record back on. She sits and listens.*

> *The sound of the scratch damage plays out. She bolts to take the record off the turntable.* GABRIEL *reappears with his manuscript in hand.*

GABRIEL: The first chapter only.

> MATILDA *removes the needle from the turntable. She puts her glasses on, with thinly veiled pride.*

MATILDA: I am going to read the absolute bejesus out of this!

> GABRIEL *withholds the manuscript. He lifts* MATILDA's *glasses off her nose, takes her in, and places the glasses back onto the bridge of her nose.*

What are you doing?

GABRIEL: Testing.

> *He again lifts her glasses on and off.*

Both adorable.

MATILDA: I cheated on the test to get my first pair, but I genuinely need these ones.

> *Beat.*

Trust me, zero façade, hand it over.

GABRIEL *hands her the manuscript.*

I Can't Write, But I Think I Am A Cat, So Read This Book Anyway by Gabriel Freeman.

Beat.

Is that really the title?

GABRIEL: Yes.

MATILDA: ... Jesus, I am going to need more than glasses.

GABRIEL: Going to bed, to count sheep, problem is it's never sheep, it's more like Tasmanian devils, the ones with that face-eating cancer—

MATILDA: Okay. Goodnight.

GABRIEL *kisses her forehead.*

GABRIEL: See you on the other side.

MATILDA: I'll call you if I need a Sherpa.

GABRIEL: Okay, Lightning Bolt.

Beat.

What? Haven't you ever had a nickname before?

MATILDA: Yes, but none of them ever fit.

Beat.

I'm convinced that man's wife sent that lightning bolt from heaven to Kempsey.

GABRIEL: People from Kempsey don't go to heaven, Matilda.

MATILDA: Go! So I can read your terrible book, you terrible, terrible person.

GABRIEL: The first chapter only.

MATILDA: Okay.

GABRIEL: Promise.

MATILDA: Promise.

GABRIEL: Then come to bed.

GABRIEL *heads toward the door. He doubles back and takes his wine. He heads to the door and hovers.*

MATILDA: ... Gabriel?

GABRIEL: I want to see if your lips move.

MATILDA: Go!

GABRIEL: 'Night 'night, Lightning Bolt.

GABRIEL *goes to leave with the bottle in hand.* MATILDA *pulls him up.*

MATILDA: Hey! Thank you.

GABRIEL: Don't thank me yet.

Gabriel's flat / Angela's flat / a restaurant.

GABRIEL *continues to make his way out. He reaches the door, and unbeknown to* MATILDA, *hovers on the edge of the room. He is joined by* TONY *and* ANGELA.

ANGELA *sits at a table fidgeting with her watch and dipping in and out of a copy of Gabriel's manuscript.*

TONY *is also holding a copy of the manuscript. He paces, occasionally stopping to support his feelings of incredulity and thinly veiled outrage.*

GABRIEL *makes his way through a bottle of wine.*

TONY, ANGELA *and* GABRIEL *speak the words* MATILDA *is reading, and true to form,* MATILDA*'s lips move as her eyes skip across the page. She also has the occasional outburst of finger tapping.*

MATILDA: [*reading*] 'To believe you are not human is a predicament for a fully grown homo sapien man.'

TONY: Here we go.

GABRIEL: 'I liked nothing more than coming home from work, locking the door and settling into a night of dressing up as a cat.'

TONY: Second sentence in and my brain is already hurting.

TONY *punches out two Panadols and swallows them.*

GABRIEL: 'Four legs, a tail, fanged teeth, the whole "catastrophe".'

TONY: Not funny, unfunny! About as funny as a Panadol, mate!

GABRIEL: 'Cat-hood was my thing. It was more than just a way of relaxing, more than an odd quirk or leftover childhood habit. I truly believed I was a cat locked in a man's body. I was not right, not right at all.'

TONY: No shit, Sherlock.

ANGELA: 'Nevertheless, she stuck by me. She tolerated my … what shall we call it … my disposition. My "cat-hood".'

TONY: This is going to bust my balls.

ANGELA: 'She would never admit it—'

GABRIEL: '—but it was my cat-like ways that attracted her to me in the first place.'

TONY: Cats lick their own arseholes, Angela, remember that!

GABRIEL *drinks.*

GABRIEL: 'My silence, my fierce independence, my hard-won affection, my nine lives. My mystery.'

TONY: Mystery? Putting tickets on yourself there, mate! We all know who you are.

GABRIEL: 'Admittedly, the mystery turned into grief when I started wearing a tail and eating out of a bowl without utensils.'

ANGELA: Jesus!

GABRIEL: '"Jesus", she would say, "Can you stop that?!" But I couldn't. And my efforts to shed my humanity became more and more humiliating. I just looked like a grown man dressed as a cat.'

ANGELA *pours a wine and drinks.*

'Needless to say, it was an unsettling condition. It had side effects.'

ANGELA: 'It became exhausting, pretending, but we had rules.'

GABRIEL: 'People would visit and say—'

TONY: '—is everything okay here?'

ANGELA: 'And we would say—'

GABRIEL: 'Yes, fine, would you like a drink, a stupid cabanossi hors d'oeuvre and some light banter about white goods followed by a surprise insult or two?'

TONY: 'Eventually people stopped coming.'

GABRIEL: 'Until it was just her and me.'

ANGELA: 'Every day she tried to remind me the human world was worth the effort, she held up little picture cards—'

ANGELA: 'Trees, grass, mountains, rain—'

TONY: Get off your arse and go outside, mate, it's all there!

GABRIEL: 'The ocean, clouds—'

TONY: All still there.

GABRIEL: 'Summer, winter—'

ANGELA: 'Day—'

GABRIEL: 'Night—'

GABRIEL: 'Rainbows—'

ANGELA: 'Clouds—'

TONY: Well, there's an error right there!

GABRIEL: 'Sunrises—'

TONY: You said clouds twice.

ANGELA: 'Sunsets, shooting stars, comets, lunar moons, blood moons, washing machines—'

ANGELA and TONY: [*together*] Washing machines?

GABRIEL: 'It all started to sound the same, even total solar eclipses that are—'

ANGELA: '—meant to bring change.'

GABRIEL: 'No matter how hard she tried, all the elements that make the world truly astonishing were lost to me.'

TONY: You want change, you stop.

ANGELA: 'Everything became a memory, and every memory became a shadow.'

TONY: Poetic way of saying he can't stop.

ANGELA: 'Minutes, days, weeks, years, were no longer held by the natural order of time and motion.'

TONY: Because he never fucking stopped.

ANGELA: 'And the loneliness of living with a half man half cat started to hollow her out.'

GABRIEL: 'Until she too crossed the precipice from love to disgust.'

TONY: Finally!

GABRIEL: 'And I was forced to admit I no longer made sense to myself.'

TONY: You can medicate animals, you know? Really, people have their cats and dogs on anti-anxiety pills, but no, let's write a two hundred … and …?

GABRIEL: 'In a final pitch at dignity I groomed my shadow, only to find everything was in the wrong place.'

TONY: Two hundred and thirteen pages, fuck me!

GABRIEL: 'There was no reference point for my being, my selfhood. So I yielded.'

ANGELA: 'To a quiet death of self-loathing.'

TONY: Self-loathing won't kill you. It just hands you the knife, mate.

    Pause. MATILDA *continues reading.*

MATILDA and GABRIEL: [*together*] One chapter, that was the deal.

MATILDA: [*reading*] 'Chapter two.'

GABRIEL: Jesus.

MATILDA: [*reading*] 'Chapter three.' 'Chapter four.'

GABRIEL: You are breaking your promises.

MATILDA: [*reading*] 'Chapter five. And with that conclusion I sensed another. The husk of existence, its voice soft and slow: "I am your shadow. I have no ears, eyes or tail. I am just your bare bones, your last chance, your end or your beginning. I don't go away, even when you can't see me. I am waiting for you. So raise your courage and look at me, because consequence will come, and it will drag you kicking and screaming to the truth of the matter." The end'

MATILDA [*reading*] and GABRIEL: [*together*] 'Come to bed now, Loved One. Brackets, Lightning Bolt.'

MATILDA: [*reading*] 'Loved One.'

> MATILDA *unwraps herself from the blanket. She is surprised to be caught by* GABRIEL, *who is still up drinking.*

GABRIEL: What did you think?

MATILDA: I thought you were going to bed. It's three a.m., Gabe.

GABRIEL: I thought you were only reading chapter one.

MATILDA: Then why did you write the footnote at the end?

GABRIEL: Thought you'd like that, Lightning Bolt.

MATILDA: At the risk of being unoriginal, I'd like you to say it.

GABRIEL: I love you, Four Eyes. There you go, got your ending.

> MATILDA *moves toward* GABRIEL. *He moves away.*

What did you think of the book?

> MATILDA *starts finger tapping.*

Come on, show me all that lost time you made up for. Go!

> *Pause.*

Fingers! Go!

MATILDA: It was good. Good?

GABRIEL: Good?

MATILDA: Yes. But I'm not sure I fully understood it. I get that life had become impossible for the cat man.

GABRIEL: Then why are you telling me you didn't understand it?

MATILDA: Because I don't know why he dresses up as a cat? I don't understand the reason.

GABRIEL: Right! So what did you come up with?

MATILDA: I don't know. That's my question—

GABRIEL: What's your question?

MATILDA: I'm not sure—

GABRIEL: Well, make some effort and be sure! Be specific. Go!

Beat.

Go!

MATILDA: I don't know …

GABRIEL: Books are propositions, Matilda, and it's the reader's job— your job is to exercise curiosity—

MATILDA: Yes, but—

GABRIEL: Curiosity, the mechanism of thinking that makes you turn the page—

MATILDA: Gabriel—

GABRIEL: But now there is a whole breed of reader that wants every stone unturned for them without ever setting foot on the path! Siri, what does this mean? Siri, what does that mean? Siri, what's the difference between my head and my arsehole?

MATILDA: Okay—

GABRIEL: I'm joking, I'm joking, Matilda.

MATILDA: Why would a man try and escape himself?

GABRIEL: What?

MATILDA: I'm being specific for you. Why was the cat man trying to escape himself?

GABRIEL: How long have you got?

MATILDA: I just gave it three hours, Gabriel. I read it from top to tail and—

GABRIEL: Want me to write another book explaining it?

MATILDA: Let's talk about it tomorrow—

GABRIEL: No.

MATILDA: You're drunk.

GABRIEL: So were you a few hours ago!

MATILDA: You have a big day tomorrow, you should—

GABRIEL: Don't tell me what I should do, the world is overpopulated, we should have done this, should have done that. You didn't like the book—

MATILDA: That's not what I said—

GABRIEL: Not as good as my first book. Doesn't raise the big questions. The 'do you think you're a worthwhile person?' question. Do you think you mean something? You know, in the greater scheme of things. Do you think you're a beautiful person? That wouldn't be a hard one for you to answer because you are truly, truly beautiful. Happy?

MATILDA: Keep your voice down—

GABRIEL: Why? The neighbours already know I am fucking someone half my age. Sorry.

> *Beat.*

You know what, I reckon I can do it. I reckon it will be easy, you won't love the bits of me you should hate. I'll break that bad habit for you, no problems. Job half done tonight, I would think. You can go if you want? You're free! Why don't you leave? Why don't you—?

MATILDA: Why don't you stop being a cunt?

GABRIEL: Well done! Want to say it again?

MATILDA: Do you do this every time someone tells you they love you?

GABRIEL: Sorry. Saying sorry. Okay?

> *Beat.*

Are you coming to bed? Or going home? I'd leave if I was you. I can't.

> *Beat.*

I'm stuck with myself. Thank you for taking the time to read my book. Good warm-up for tomorrow.

MATILDA: What?

GABRIEL: You wanted in. Got what you want now? Good enough for you?

> GABRIEL *exits.* MATILDA *picks up her handbag, sits down, stands up, sits down again. She gathers herself and exits.*

SCENE THREE—THE VERDICT

A restaurant. GABRIEL *sits opposite* ANGELA. *A table, a bottle of wine and Gabriel's manuscript sit between them.*

GABRIEL: Hello.
ANGELA: No.
GABRIEL: Okay.

He pours himself a drink. Pause.

Don't cry.

ANGELA *picks up a napkin.*

ANGELA: Don't flatter yourself.

ANGELA *cleans her glasses with the napkin.*

GABRIEL: Okay.
ANGELA: Don't smile at me, Gabriel.
GABRIEL: Okay.
ANGELA: I want to look at you for a while.
GABRIEL: Okay.
ANGELA: Without smiling or talking or some fantasy about me crying. So whatever shit is going on in your head, shut it down. I am not interested.
GABRIEL: Nice to see you too.
ANGELA: Shut up.

Silence.

GABRIEL: You just let me know when you're ready—
ANGELA: Shut up. It is the least you could do.

Pause.

GABRIEL: How you going, Angie?

Pause.

You know they have a world championship in staring—?
ANGELA: Shut up!
GABRIEL: Somewhere in Scandinavia—
ANGELA: You've never liked being too closely observed, have you?
GABRIEL: You know me.

Silence. ANGELA *touches his left cheek.*

Did that help?
ANGELA: None of your business.

Pause.

GABRIEL: I feel a little bit uneven, why don't you do the other side?

ANGELA *slaps his right cheek.*

Jesus!

ANGELA: Are you real, are you a real person, Gabe?

GABRIEL: Yes, and I know this to be true because that slap actually hurt.

GABRIEL *drinks and tops up his wine.*

ANGELA: How is the wine?

GABRIEL: Can we be civil?

ANGELA: I am. How is the wine?

GABRIEL: Good! Thank you.

ANGELA: I took your cat.

GABRIEL: It was your cat.

ANGELA: He was hanging round your door, day after day, but like everyone that waits for you, he just got sick and tired and thin.

GABRIEL: You were the first one to leave, Ange, remember that—

ANGELA: No, I just got out of the way so you could stay up all night—

GABRIEL: Okay—

ANGELA: Sleep all day, piss your life away—

GABRIEL: Okay—

ANGELA: Piss the bed! Piss all over the page and pretend you're writing.

Beat.

Two years?

Beat.

GABRIEL: I'm well, thank you for asking.

ANGELA: You look terrible.

GABRIEL: Thanks. You look great.

ANGELA: You look the same, Gabriel.

GABRIEL: Jesus.

Beat.

ANGELA: Tony's allergic to the cat.

GABRIEL: What?

ANGELA: Tony is allergic to your arsehole cat!

Beat.

GABRIEL: Tony?

ANGELA: Yes. Tony

GABRIEL: … Okay.

> *Beat.*

… Tony?

ANGELA: Yes?

GABRIEL: Friendly Tony?

ANGELA: Yes. Friendly Tony.

> *Beat.*

Friendly, loving, trustworthy, kind Tony.

GABRIEL: Accountant Tony?

ANGELA: Yes, were you under the delusion I would wait for you?

> *Beat.*

What do you want, Gabe?

> *Beat.*

GABRIEL: I can take the cat back if—

ANGELA: No, we've grown attached to hating him. Two years. Your phone was dead, I asked your friends, your doctor. I filed you as a missing person, Gabe—a missing person …

> *Beat.*

I went to your mother's funeral, Gabriel.

GABRIEL: How were the speeches?

> *Beat.*

Did they say she was a good person?

ANGELA: Don't know, I couldn't hear anything, couldn't see anything. I … I got fucking hijacked by the thought that you were dead.

GABRIEL: Sorry.

> *Beat.*

ANGELA: She was eighty-four, unable to swallow—

GABRIEL: I said goodbye before I left. I leaned right in and asked, 'Do you think I am a worthwhile human being, Mum?' And guess what she said.

ANGELA: …?

GABRIEL: 'No hard questions.'

> *Beat.*

Imagine if I had have turned up. The rage would've brought her back to life. 'Why is he wearing that? Why is he sitting there? Why is he thinking that? Why did they let him inside a church?'

ANGELA: Stop—

GABRIEL: 'Why isn't he crying? Why are his books full of cursing? Why did he write all those horrible truths about me? And why am I dead when I still have so much criticism left to give? Where is that lovely girl Angela? There she is! Front row centre, suffering through it, loving what we couldn't.'

Pause.

I was missing from everybody, Angie, not just you. I went missing from myself, I needed a re-set so I re-set. I sent you an email.

ANGELA: 'I am still on this planet. It is a dark season. I shan't be sharing. Be patient. Regards, G.' 'Regards'? What is that? I thought you might be dead, Gabriel.

GABRIEL: No, I'm alive. And slappable. Come on, Angie—

ANGELA: What were you thinking?

GABRIEL: I wasn't well enough to think! Alright! It's like a hard drive, you just keep putting stuff on it, more and more stuff on it, and … and one day it just breaks. The computer shits itself.

ANGELA: But you managed to write a book.

GABRIEL: Have you read it?

ANGELA: Oh, fuck off.

GABRIEL: Did you like it?

ANGELA: Really, go and get fucked!

GABRIEL: I am, thank you.

Beat.

ANGELA: I thought you were meant to start with a pot plant?

GABRIEL: I did. It died.

ANGELA: What flavour of disposable goods did you—?

GABRIEL: She's lovely.

ANGELA: We are all lovely in the beginning, lovely and all so sorry for you.

GABRIEL: I don't need you to be lovely or sorry for me. I need you to tell me what you think of my book?

ANGELA: Cat stuck inside a man's body? It's clever with zero integrity.

GABRIEL: Are you going to publish it?

ANGELA: No.

GABRIEL: I just need an edit—

ANGELA: I need! I need an explanation! Where have you've been?

GABRIEL: I'm not your problem anymore, Angela.

ANGELA: So what are we doing here? You can't write a book every time you run out of money and love, Gabe, doesn't work that way.

GABRIEL: I'm letting you know I am okay.

ANGELA: You're not okay.

GABRIEL: Can we talk about the book?

ANGELA: Sure. It's shit. Cat stuck inside a man's body? It's a shit version of your first novel, like all your books, except this one is shitter than the last one. If you want to be clever with words, and seduce people, become a copy writer.

GABRIEL: And now you've got the constructive criticism out of your system, you can tell me what you liked about it and when you are going to publish it.

ANGELA: If I liked it I'd tell you to take it to someone else, but you'll just prolong the agony, because it is truly shit. You'll just get rejected, drink more, get rejected, drink more and so on. Save some time, cut yourself off at the knees now and learn how to walk again.

GABRIEL: I'm here, aren't I?

ANGELA: No. You're a bottle down. I know that look, your left dimple disappears, and you blink less. It is like you live in a parallel universe, where you are the only one who hasn't cottoned on to the fact you are a human living alongside other humans and—

GABRIEL: Come on, Angie. There is no other way for us to do this. We owe it, we owe it to our past.

ANGELA: What?

GABRIEL: There is no other way to do this—You're just going to run out of steam running round being angry with me and pretending you never loved me. You may as well stop wasting your time and jump in the deep end now.

Pause.

ANGELA: The deep end? Okay.

She hands GABRIEL *a photo. He looks at it.*

GABRIEL: See, I did you a favour, I disappear and all of a sudden your dreams come true. Where is it?

ANGELA: You're holding it upside down.

GABRIEL: South Coast?

ANGELA: No.

GABRIEL: Tasmania?

ANGELA: It's not land, Gabriel.

GABRIEL: I thought it was an aerial shot …

ANGELA: Put your glasses on. Stop pretending you can see properly.

> GABRIEL *put his glasses on. Silence.*

Two months and two days.

GABRIEL: Boy or a girl?

ANGELA: A girl.

GABRIEL: Congratulations.

ANGELA: I wrote to you—

GABRIEL: Sorry, I stopped reading emails.

> *Beat.*

I am happy for you, Angie.

ANGELA: Edward syndrome. An extra copy of chromosome eighteen. They offered me a counsellor, but you know me, Wikipedia, on my mobile phone in the hospital car park. And of course, the older you are the more likely this—it—if I gave birth …

> *Pause.* GABRIEL *offers her a napkin. She does not take it.*

If I gave birth, the survival rates are ninety percent don't make it to a year. Fifty percent die in the first week

> *Beat.*

I miscarried one day after I made the decision to have a termination. I went to bed for a week. Tony sat hunched over a calculator, drinking black coffee, tying to work out if we could afford to try again. I was done. You asked for the deep end. You wouldn't know what the deep end was if someone held you down and drowned you in it. How old is your new girlfriend?

GABRIEL: Angie …

ANGELA: How old is she, Gabe?

> *Beat.*

How old—?

GABRIEL: Twenty-four.

ANGELA: Right.

> *Beat.*

I wanted a child. I still want a child. I can't stop wanting a child and I am never going to have a child. Give me that napkin.

GABRIEL: I'm sorry—

ANGELA: 'If Gabriel really loved you, he'd go to AA and get himself cured. Shame you're such a pretty girl.' I think that was the cruelest thing your mother ever said to me. Problem with cruel people is they often tell the truth. There are a lot of people in the world whose parents didn't love them, Gabe. I'm sure it leaves a big dent, but they get on with life. You're forty-eight. Grieve, or have another drink. Up to you. I don't care anymore.

> *She tops up* GABRIEL's *wine.*

No?

> ANGELA *drinks the wine, then refills the glass.*

GABRIEL: What are you doing, Angela?

> *Pause.*

ANGELA: I am allowing myself to hate you.

> *Beat.*

Towards the end it was automatic. I could step over you passed out in the corridor without even looking down.

> ANGELA *drinks another glass of wine. She closes her eyes and reaches her hand across the table till she finds* GABRIEL's *face. She feels it like it is made of play dough.*

GABRIEL: Stop it.

> ANGELA *continues to blindly feel his face.*

ANGELA: 'You're okay.'

GABRIEL: Angie—

ANGELA: 'You'll be okay. Go back to sleep.'

> GABRIEL's *tolerance breaks and he grabs* ANGELA's *hand.*

GABRIEL: Enough!

ANGELA: Yes it was.

> *Beat.*

When your time comes, I'll stand on your grave and drink a bottle of champagne.

SCENE FOUR—WAR AND PEACE

Gabriel's flat.

GABRIEL: Champagne!
MATILDA: It went well?
GABRIEL: It's French—
MATILDA: Did it go—?
GABRIEL: Yes.
MATILDA: Well?
GABRIEL: I said yes.
MATILDA: It went well?
GABRIEL: But that is not what the champagne is for. It's for you.
MATILDA: Is she going to publish your book?
GABRIEL: Think so.
MATILDA: You think so, or you know so?
GABRIEL: She'll publish it.
MATILDA: When?
GABRIEL: These things take time.
MATILDA: How much time?
GABRIEL: Matilda …
MATILDA: She liked it?
GABRIEL: Yes.
MATILDA: What did she say?
GABRIEL: She said it was clever and it has integrity.
MATILDA: That sounds like a contradiction.
GABRIEL: She said it would seduce people. She might want me to change a thing or two.
MATILDA: Like what?
GABRIEL: Small details.
MATILDA: The title?
GABRIEL: No.
MATILDA: What?

GABRIEL: Just …
MATILDA: What?
GABRIEL: Just a little edit, it's normal.

Beat.

MATILDA: Is she going to come to dinner?
GABRIEL: Not sure. She has to talk to her partner.
MATILDA: She has a—
GABRIEL: Yes.
MATILDA: You never told—
GABRIEL: I didn't know! We don't—I don't—we're not—This champagne is for you.
MATILDA: You already told me that. Did you even ask her to dinner?
GABRIEL: Yes. They'll let us know.
MATILDA: Tell me exactly what she said about the book.
GABRIEL: She said it was clever.
MATILDA: You already told me that. What else did she say?
GABRIEL: Jesus, Matilda!

Beat.

I got you a present.
MATILDA: I bet you did.

GABRIEL *produces a present.*

GABRIEL: What's wrong?
MATILDA: Do you remember what you said last night?
GABRIEL: I let you read my book, I remember that.
MATILDA: But you don't remember being a cunt?

Beat.

GABRIEL: No.
MATILDA: No?

Beat.

Do you think you're a worthwhile person, Gabriel?
GABRIEL: Well, I was a cunt a second ago, so I'm not sure I understand the context of the question, Matilda.

Pause. GABRIEL *refers to the present.*

You going to open that?

MATILDA *opens her present. It is a hard copy of* War and Peace. *She is unmoved. Pause.*

War and Peace.

MATILDA: The thing that really got me is you said the neighbours knew you were sleeping—sorry, fucking someone half your age, like I am some sort of walking talking fuckable defamation on your character. I've read this.

GABRIEL: I thought you said *Crime*—

MATILDA: I've read both.

Beat.

And the other one ... *Anna* ... whatsaname?

GABRIEL: *Karenina.*

MATILDA: Her. Don't underestimate me, Gabriel.

Pause.

GABRIEL: I have no doubt I was an arsehole. Okay. It is French. Sorry. Okay?

MATILDA: Take me out.

GABRIEL: What?

MATILDA: We never go out. I need to go—we need to get out of this flat—

GABRIEL: I got stuff for dinner.

MATILDA: No you didn't, you ordered it online. You don't leave the flat except to see her! Every night we sit here—I can't ... I need to get—we need to go out!

GABRIEL: Can we finish the champagne first?

MATILDA: Where's your life? Is it really this small? You don't do anything, Gabe. What do you do? Did you ask her to dinner?

GABRIEL: Yes, Jesus. Matilda, give me a break, okay. I wasn't kidding about the two years alone—

MATILDA: You floated round Asia, using your mother's inheritance and wrote a book. Want a medal for having the luxury of dipping out of the real world? She can go do her edit of your clever book and it can be a big success. Like your first book. But in the meantime the real world is waiting for you. I am waiting for you, Gabe. When you're lying on your deathbed will you be thinking about all the books you've written or will you be thinking about the people you loved, or failed to love? You are the one that needs to think. Wake up!

Beat.

Christ! Can we just get out, go out? I want to go out!

GABRIEL: Where?

MATILDA: A movie, a walk, a swim, Christ ... mini-fucking-golf, anything! I don't care, surprise me, I need you to surprise me. You're still in love with her, aren't you?

Beat.

Please surprise me, Gabe. I need you to surprise me.

GABRIEL: Hey—

MATILDA: I'm pregnant.

Pause.

I'm pregnant.

Pause.

Pregnant—

GABRIEL: Just give me a minute here—fuck ... okay.

Beat.

My heart hurts—okay, my—I'm not kidding, Matilda, my actual heart is hurting.

MATILDA: Good! But don't have a heart attack on me, you're not having a heart attack on me, are you?

GABRIEL: No, I just—it's—I swear to God, it's like, like you said. I can feel all my internal organs.

MATILDA: Two weeks—

GABRIEL: Two weeks.

MATILDA: Then eight months and two weeks. Then a lifetime.

GABRIEL: Okay. Okay, so you are going to—

MATILDA: Yes!

GABRIEL: Okay ... big news. Okay.

MATILDA: Okay?

Pause.

I thought about your question. I am a worthwhile human being.

GABRIEL: I know that. I'm sorry.

MATILDA: So get your shit together, get—get right.

GABRIEL: Right?

MATILDA: Yeah, right!

Beat.

'Adorable—a term used to describe people or animals that are easy to love because they are so attractive and often small.' Nothing about façade. I looked it up. You are going to have to stop drinking.

SCENE FIVE—FRIENDLY TONY

Tony and Angela's flat. TONY *reads from Gabriel's manuscript.*

TONY: [*reading*] 'And with that conclusion I sensed another, the husk of a stranger's existence'—Better late than never. So what was it this time? Has he found God?

ANGELA: No.

TONY: No? No, well let's face it God would struggle to find him.

ANGELA: Why don't you just ask me?

TONY: Sure. Not a problem—

ANGELA: He repulses me.

TONY: Not what I was going to ask.

Beat.

Did he say sorry again?

ANGELA: No.

TONY: Right.

Pause.

So?

ANGELA: He is not sober, Tony.

TONY: Oh, I jumped a step. Sorry. I always underestimate how much I should underestimate him. Let's go back a few steps. So, what did he want?

ANGELA: To let me know he was alright.

TONY: What did he want, Angela?

ANGELA: Nothing.

TONY: What did he—?

ANGELA: He wanted to see if I would publish his book.

TONY: There you go! Was that so hard? Anything else?

ANGELA: No.

TONY: Nothing?

ANGELA: Tony …?

TONY: Well, that is unusual. You'd have to agree, that is unusual—

ANGELA: Don't—

TONY: After all those things you used to do—

ANGELA: Stop it—

TONY: The gift buying, the money giving, the excuse making. The appointment making, the job hunting, the flat hunting, calling his ex-friends, driving him everywhere, paying his bills, trying to make him eat, sleep, bathe! The excuses that you repeated so many times, you ended up convincing yourself they were the truth. The health farms! Him sitting in a spa bath on your coin, convincing himself that he was doing well because the wine was organic and the people were nice. Packing up his life for him when he decides to vanish. Christ! And last but not least, sitting at his mother's deathbed. And the irony is you wanted a child, when you never stopped behaving like his mother. What would be the point of him apologising again? Last time he said sorry he disappeared for two years, just to give you room to feel sorry for him all over again. And let's not forget his trump card, his ability to keep you up at night, worrying he might be dead. Again. Next time he wants to kill himself he should invite me round—sorry—see this is what he does, this is who he makes us, who he makes me. I almost admire his consistency, Angela, but not yours.

ANGELA: You're being cruel now.

TONY: It hurts for a reason, Ange.

Pause.

Are you going to publish his book?

Beat.

Are you going to publish his book?

ANGELA: No!

TONY *sneezes.*

Bless you—

TONY *sneezes again.*

TONY: That fucking cat! Christ!

ANGELA: Take an antihistamine.

TONY: No!

Beat.

I can see it in your face, Angela. Why did you bother telling me? Did you want to see what my face would look like when I know you've seen him? Well, here it is. It looks like this. Christ! Would you have even told me he was back? If I didn't see his book on your desk—

He sneezes once more.

Is he going to take the cat back?

ANGELA: No. It's our cat now.

TONY: We don't even like cats, Angela!

ANGELA: I watched that animal slowly forget him and it gave me comfort.

TONY: Am I a comfort too? Everything, every little thing is in relation to him, I saved you from him, the cat helps you forget him, we might have a child because he sure as hell couldn't. Bury the hatchet, or pick it up and bludgeon him to death with it.

Beat.

ANGELA: He has a girlfriend.

TONY: Good luck to her.

Beat.

ANGELA: She's twenty-four.

TONY: So? Did you tell him?

ANGELA: No.

TONY: You're lying. You would have told him.

ANGELA: Why would I tell him?

TONY: To get him to feel something about you. Feel sorry for you, anything, just to get him to feeling something about you. You're as addicted as him, Angie.

ANGELA: What do I have to do?

TONY: Tell the truth.

ANGELA: I am telling the truth. You need to trust me. I want you to trust me.

She kisses him. The kissing moves into foreplay. TONY *abruptly breaks away, with his hand to his mouth.*

TONY: What the fuck?

ANGELA: Sorry.

TONY: Why did you do that?

ANGELA: Sorry.

TONY: You bit me—

ANGELA: Sorry—I don't—sorry—

TONY: Shit ...? What did you do that for?

ANGELA: I don't know—

TONY: Jesus, Angela.

ANGELA: I'm sorry.

TONY: Why did you do that?

ANGELA: I don't know.

TONY: Yes you do.

He holds up his finger. It has blood on it from where ANGELA *bit him.*

This is us.

ANGELA: Let me help you—

TONY: Help me by listening to me. Hear this and know it, take it in, right in, put it in your marrow, sweetheart. Let go of him. Not just because the child we lost was never going to have to step over me passed out in the hallway, not because I was going to love that child more than my next drink, more than my next book, or whatever you call that drunken scribble he regurgitates, not just because I am here, and I will always be here. Because—stop this—stop!

Beat.

Cat stuck inside a man's body, fucking hell!

ANGELA: You read the whole thing?

TONY: Yes. I did, Angela! What about a man stuck inside an alcoholic's body? No-one would buy that one, would they? Except you. You know what the pathetic thing is? I am terrified that the only thing that stands between you and him is sobriety.

ANGELA: I've made up my mind.

TONY: Make up your heart, Angela, that's the part I want. You would have told him because it would be easier if he was the only one to blame. You left it too late to have children. You did that, not him. You stayed with him, your mistake. Your mistake! Don't expect me to pay the price. Change, if you can't, leave me.

Beat.

What do you want to do?

ANGELA: I am not going back. I am never going back. I can't—
TONY: I am fully aware you can't tolerate him.
ANGELA: I hate him.
TONY: Yep, I think you do.

TONY *gets up to leave.*

ANGELA: Where are you going?
TONY: For a drive.

Pause.

Jesus, Angela.

ANGELA: What do you want me to do?
TONY: People think love is the opposite of hate. They're wrong.
ANGELA: I don't know what you want me to do?
TONY: Indifference is the opposite of love, Angela.
ANGELA: I am not indifferent.
TONY: Then get on your knees and beg me to stay. See how it feels down here.

Beat.

Didn't think so.

SCENE SIX—NON FICTION

GABRIEL *is now reading* Men Without Women. MATILDA *sits opposite, staring at him.* GABRIEL *speaks to her without abandoning his book.*

GABRIEL: … Yes? Lightning Bolt?
MATILDA: Is your first book fiction, Gabriel?
GABRIEL: What?
MATILDA: Is your first book fiction?

Beat.

GABRIEL: That's a very unoriginal question for a Monday evening, Matilda.

MATILDA: Unoriginal because it's true?

GABRIEL: Go into any bookstore and it's under fiction.

MATILDA: I'm not asking the bookstore, I am asking you.

GABRIEL: Stop interrupting the sacred bond between man and Hemingway.

Pause.

MATILDA: You don't write a book like that when you're seventeen without having some level of experience. Is it—?

GABRIEL: You've read too many reviews. Are you joining the pack and accusing me of having no imagination?

MATILDA: No—

GABRIEL: So what are you doing?

MATILDA: You could just answer my question, Gabriel.

GABRIEL: And you could not insult me by asking the question.

MATILDA: If you're going to be a father—

GABRIEL: Don't play that card.

MATILDA: I am trying to understand—

GABRIEL: And what are you going to do if and when you understand? You have some fairy dust hidden away in your arsenal that can erase the past? Or can you raise my parents from the dead and hold them accountable? Present the case to them: 'Mr Freeman, did you really tell your son to jump out of a tree and promise you'd catch him, then sit beside him in hospital and say, "Let that be a lesson to you to never trust anyone, and don't always do what people tell you to"? Mr Freeman, did you throw your son's pet out the window of a three-storey building because it shat in your perfect pristine academic study?'

MATILDA: I've read the book.

GABRIEL: According to the book, the cat died on impact and the father wasn't an academic. The theory is right, you can drop a cat from a great height, and it will survive. But if it's a four-month-old kitten, it will break its leg and its lungs will collapse. My father didn't believe in paying money for what he could do himself, he euthanased the cat with his left foot. And my mother dutifully cleaned his boots after the event without a fucking peep. Teamwork. The clever thing about my parents was they never laid a finger on me. Bruises would have been embarrassing for sophisticates like them. It has been a while since I read the book, so correct me if I am wrong, I believe I wrote parents that beat the crap out of their child. So, to answer your question, the book is fiction. Sorry to disappoint you. Where are your fingers, I thought they'd be tapping by now? You want me not to drink then don't ferret around and make me feel sick. By the way that cat my father killed was a birthday present. Don't ask questions you don't want the answer to.

GABRIEL goes back to his book. Silence.

MATILDA: Gabriel—

GABRIEL: I have days you know, days where I hate Hemingway with all my heart. Tricky, that thing, where you hate the thing you're meant to love.

GABRIEL abruptly gets up and exits. He returns with a bottle of wine and a glass of wine. He resumes reading.

MATILDA: What are you doing?

GABRIEL: I am doing my best, let me be the judge of what that is.

He goes back to his book. Pause.

What are you reading?

MATILDA: Gabriel—

GABRIEL: Don't, okay.

Beat.

MATILDA: I think I'll go home.

GABRIEL: At this time of night? Okay, Lightning Bolt.

Beat.

Call me when you get there, to let me know you're safe.

Beat.

Well, are you going or not? Stop wanting me to be something I'm not because this is it, okay.

Beat.

Christ! Do you want me to open the door for you!

MATILDA exits, taking Gabriel's bottle of wine with her. A defeated GABRIEL pauses, then moves towards his bedroom with purpose.

SCENE SEVEN—DEAD CAT

Tony and Angela's flat. TONY *comes striding in. He is agitated. He makes a beeline for the Scotch.*

ANGELA: Where did you go?
TONY: Do you want a drink?
ANGELA: Yes … no. Yes—no—
TONY: Do you want a—?
ANGELA: I said no. Long drive. Where did you go?

> TONY *necks a Scotch and sits. Silence.*

TONY: It was an accident.
ANGELA: What?

> TONY *gets up and is on the move, he can't stand still.*

TONY: I swear it was—
ANGELA: What happened?
TONY: You're not going to believe me—
ANGELA: Your nose is bleeding
TONY: I swear it was an accident.

> *Beat.*

ANGELA: What happened?

> *Beat.*

TONY: I ran over the cat.
ANGELA: … What?
TONY: The little shit ran out—
ANGELA: Okay—
TONY: Onto the road—
ANGELA: No.

> *Beat.*

It's okay.
TONY: It's not okay.

> *Beat.*

I killed it.

> *Beat.*

ANGELA: Good.

TONY: It's dead.

ANGELA: Good.

TONY: ... Dead.

ANGELA: Come here, let me look at your nose—

TONY: The car's fucked.

ANGELA: What?

TONY: I swerved to miss the cat and the car just ... I ran into a tree!

ANGELA: Your ear's bleeding.

TONY: ... What?

ANGELA: There's blood—sit down—

TONY: All I could think was—

ANGELA: There's blood coming out—

TONY: —don't kill that little shit—

ANGELA: Sit down—

TONY: Next thing I know I have a fucking tree coming at me!

ANGELA: Please sit—

TONY: Don't leave me.

ANGELA: Let me look at you—

TONY: Please don't leave me. It's just a scratch.

ANGELA: Tony—

TONY: Don't leave me. Promise me.

He collapses into a chair.

If there was one thing I could change about myself, it would be loving you. I would not be in love with you—

ANGELA: There's blood coming out of your ear, Tony—

TONY *touches the blood coming from his ear. He holds up his hand as* ANGELA *approaches him.*

TONY: Don't come near me.

SCENE EIGHT—THE BURIAL

GABRIEL *is on the floor, he is clearly unwell.* ANGELA *enters and drops a shovel at his feet.*

ANGELA: Get up.

GABRIEL: I can't.

ANGELA: Get up.

GABRIEL: My legs are not working.

ANGELA: Get up—

GABRIEL: I can't!

ANGELA: I don't give a fuck about what you can't do anymore. Get up.

SCEEN NINE—THE TIPPING POINT

Gabriel's flat. GABRIEL *is on the floor. He is covered in dirt. A shovel is on the floor beside him.* MATILDA *observes him from a distance.*

GABRIEL: Don't.

MATILDA: Don't what?

GABRIEL: Don't look at me, and don't do the other the thing—you're doing right now, being right, you're always right. Don't be so good at being right. It's unattractive.

> GABRIEL *gets up.*

MATILDA: Sit down—

GABRIEL: Calm down—

MATILDA: I am calm, Gabriel—

GABRIEL: Calm down, and get me a glass of water. Please.

> MATILDA *gets* GABRIEL *a glass of water. Pause.*

MATILDA: The kitchen smells of gas, Gabriel?

GABRIEL: I know, I fucked it, but my socks are matching, look!

> GABRIEL *makes his way around the room using the wall to hold his balance. His hands leave dirt handprints on the wall.*

MATILDA: Don't you want the water?

> *Beat.*

You're putting dirt all over the wall. Why are you covered in dirt, Gabe?

GABRIEL: I am made of dirt.

> *Beat.*

MATILDA: I am going to take you to hospital.

GABRIEL: Tomorrow.

> GABRIEL *makes his way out of the room.* MATILDA *waits.* GABRIEL *returns with a bottle of wine. He slides down the wall.*

MATILDA *takes the wine off him and places the glass of water in his hand. He hesitates and pours it over his head. Pause.*

You like that?

MATILDA: No—

GABRIEL: Yes you do. Because you are one of them. One of those people who think that I have a drinking problem—

MATILDA: You do have a drinking problem—

GABRIEL: No—

MATILDA: Then why have you pissed your pants, Gabriel?

GABRIEL: My problem is not drinking. My problem is being sober. I am not the sickness, let us be clear. The sickness is not me. Not me!

MATILDA: Yes it is, Gabe.

MATILDA *starts to leave.*

GABRIEL: Don't—do not leave me.

He catches her ankle. She freezes.

Sorry, sorry, sorry.

MATILDA: You make a decision. I take you to hospital. Not tomorrow, now. Or you never see me again. Make a—

GABRIEL: Hello, this is an emergency, I pissed my pants. Calm down.

MATILDA: I have to go—

GABRIEL: I don't know how to do it—

MATILDA: What?

GABRIEL: I don't know how to keep living.

Beat.

MATILDA: You make a decision. You get in the car and we go to hospital.

GABRIEL: I can't.

MATILDA: Yes you can. You start by taking my hand. And then we walk to the door. And then we get in the car.

She holds out her hand.

Take my hand.

He takes her hand.

GABRIEL: I'm sorry.

MATILDA: Walk.

GABRIEL: Sorry—

MATILDA: Walk. Don't you dare apologise to me and not keep walking. Walk.

SCENE TEN—THE ART OF ACCEPTING FLOWERS

A hospital.

MATILDA *is holding a bunch of flowers.* ANGELA *looks at her like she's an alien.*

MATILDA: Matilda.
ANGELA: Who—?
MATILDA: Gabriel's girlfriend—
ANGELA: Right.
MATILDA: For you.
ANGELA: What are you doing here?
MATILDA: I was just going to leave them at the front desk but the nurse just—she pointed you out and … Would you like me to put them in water?
ANGELA: No!
MATILDA: Okay.

Pause.

Is there anything I can do?

Beat.

ANGELA: Ask me how he is.
MATILDA: … Sorry.

Beat.

How is he—?
ANGELA: He's had a cerebral bleed. His brain is swollen. He's unconscious. And the doctors, the only people that can know, don't know … They do know the damage is significant.
MATILDA: I'm sorry.

Pause.

Anything I can do, really anything—
ANGELA: Like what?

Beat.

MATILDA: … If you needed lifts or—

ANGELA: Lifts?

MATILDA: Home or back here.

ANGELA: I can drive.

MATILDA: ... No, of course, but if you need anything dropped off or picked up or ...?

ANGELA: Or?

MATILDA: ... Anything. If you think of anything.

Pause.

I'd be—

ANGELA: I'm thinking.

MATILDA: Sorry.

ANGELA: Because I would really like to come up with something, given I can't take back time. He was just going out for a drive, he was just driving like every other day.

Beat.

MATILDA: I'd be happy to do anything I could.

ANGELA: Make me less fucking furious.

Pause.

MATILDA: Would you like a tea or a coffee? I can do that.

ANGELA: No.

MATILDA: [*the flowers*] They are from both of us.

ANGELA: You know what one of the causes of a brain haemorrhage can be, besides a traumatic blow to the head? Liver disease. Ironic, don't you think? Running into a tree to avoid a cat is rare. Very rare. What do you want?

MATILDA: Could you ... I think it would be good if Gabriel knew you could ...

ANGELA: What?

Pause.

MATILDA: Forgive him. Not that it's his fault. But he's in rehab and—I ... I need everything, everything I can get to—to make him well, so if you could—

ANGELA: A tip for you, it is Gabriel's right to drink. It is his right to drink himself to death if he wants to. I suggest you allow him the dignity of the choice. I never did. That bit they say about them having to want to get well, that's true.

MATILDA: Sorry, I should't have asked.

ANGELA: Keep the flowers. They're everywhere, bunches upon bunches of them. I can barely get in the room. By the time Tony wakes up they will be dead.

Beat.

He is going to wake up.

Beat.

Do you know what the most forgiving organ in the body is?

MATILDA: No?

ANGELA: Guess.

MATILDA: The heart.

ANGELA: No.

Beat.

MATILDA: I hope Tony is … I truly, with all my heart, really with every inch of it. I … I hope he recovers. And I am sorry for what is happening to you.

Beat.

I still don't understand how you could make Gabriel dig a grave for a cat when he had just tried to kill himself.

Beat.

ANGELA: Most days he just drip-feeds you crisis, until it slowly becomes the norm. He can gas himself or kill himself by increments, I am at the stage where I find it hard to separate the two.

Beat.

These flowers aren't for me. You brought them to make yourself feel better. Keep them. I don't want to take anything from you. So I think that's us done.

MATILDA: Did he tell you I was pregnant?

ANGELA: Sorry?

MATILDA: Because I am. Pregnant.

Beat.

Only two weeks, but—

ANGELA: Sit down.

Pause.

This is going to be hard for me. So make up your mind. Sit down and listen to me or leave.

Beat. MATILDA *sits.* ANGELA *sits beside her.*

When I was nine weeks pregnant, I woke up in the middle of the night. I tried to wake Gabriel. Again, and again, and again, and in that again and again, I realised four months sober was over. When he eventually woke up, I told him I thought I was losing our child and he … he … without opening his eyes, he reached out and felt my face, like it was a piece of Play-Doh. And he said, 'You're okay. Shhhhhh, you'll be okay. Go back to sleep.' Our neighbour drove me to hospital. Gabriel and I walked round the house like ghosts, unable to look at each other for days. A week after I lost my child, he arrived home with a kitten, and its name tag was engraved 'Sorry'. Drunks are creative. I'll give him that. I left him and the cat that night. And I took the bar with me because I wanted to make sure he knew I was gone. Don't for a minute think I told you this to hurt you.

Pause.

Are you cat or a dog person?

MATILDA: Dog.

ANGELA: You should get one. Once things … when your baby is born and you're settled. Get a dog. Get things in your life that you can love.

Beat.

The most forgiving organ in the body is the liver. It will out-forgive you. Don't waste your time waiting for things to change. You stay with him you will just become the bookend for his bullshit, his cruelty and his inability to love.

ANGELA *exits.*

SCENE ELEVEN—BARE BONES

A rehab.

MATILDA *is unloading a bag of items for* GABRIEL. *It includes jelly babies, a Toblerone and Coca-Cola.* GABRIEL *is currently a one out of ten.*

MATILDA: If you don't want them you can just give them to someone else, I'm sure there are other people here that you could give them to. I won't take it personally, I—

GABRIEL: Am I seeing things or is that Toblerone massive?

MATILDA: It's a bonus value bar. Limited Edition. It was on special. You don't have to eat it all at once—

GABRIEL: It's massive. It's fucking massive.

MATILDA: I know, but the thing is there is more space between the triangles, so it's not really bigger, it is just designed to look bigger, the peak is higher but the base is narrower, there is more air between each piece and the packaging is—

GABRIEL: Shhhhhhh.

MATILDA: Sorry.

> *Pause.*

How are you?

GABRIEL: On valium. You?

> GABRIEL *tries to open the jelly babies. His hands are shaking, he struggles.*

MATILDA: I'll do it.

> *She opens it and hands it back.* GABRIEL *eats one or two jelly babies whilst* MATILDA *continues to unpack sweet treats, toiletries and ice cream.*

Is there a fridge?

GABRIEL: …?

MATILDA: Ice cream.

> GABRIEL *takes the ice cream and starts to exit. He drops the ice cream.* MATILDA *rises.* GABRIEL *puts his hand out to stop her. Pause.* GABRIEL *leaves the ice cream, doubles back and hugs* MATILDA. GABRIEL *exits, picking up the ice cream on the way out.*

Gabe?

> GABRIEL *holds up the ice cream without turning back.*

GABRIEL: Fridge.

> MATILDA *sits, her aloneness is acute. She takes in her surroundings, they upset her. She works hard to suppress her grief.* GABRIEL

returns with two spoons and the ice cream. He notes MATILDA*'s distress.*

MATILDA: No fridge?

GABRIEL: Spoons.

GABRIEL *struggles to get the lid off the ice cream.*

MATILDA: I'll do it.

GABRIEL: Jesus, Matilda! Please! ... Sorry. I'm really sorry.

MATILDA: It's okay.

He finally gets the lid off. He hands her a spoon.

GABRIEL: Have some ice cream.

MATILDA *has some ice cream. Silence.*

You'll like this, essentially there is not such a big age gap between us. I haven't really been sober for thirty-three years. So according to this place I'm still sixteen. So don't expect ... Thank you for the ice cream. I don't know if I can do this.

MATILDA: One day at a time.

GABRIEL: And all those days will add up to nine months and—

MATILDA: And life will still be one day at a time.

She unwraps the Toblerone. She examines the bar.

See, they cheated on the base—

GABRIEL: I don't know if I can do this.

MATILDA: You already said that. And between the first and the second time you said it, you haven't had a drink, so you are doing this.

Silence.

You have to want something, Gabe.

GABRIEL: I know.

MATILDA: Something to get well for.

GABRIEL: Have you read every pamphlet in this place?

MATILDA: You have to have hope.

Pause.

GABRIEL: Story?

MATILDA: Sure.

GABRIEL: This one is going to feel a little different.

MATILDA: Okay.

GABRIEL: It's your favourite genre—

MATILDA: Tortured Russian.

GABRIEL: No. Just true.

MATILDA: Okay.

GABRIEL: A few years back, I found my cat with a bird in his mouth.

MATILDA: Cats are cunts, they kill native wildlife, they shit in trays, hiss, show people their cunting entitled teeth and—

GABRIEL: Hello! There you are! Thought you'd never arrive.

MATILDA: Sorry. I interrupted, sorry.

> *Beat.*

Sorry.

GABRIEL: Stop being sorry, Matilda!

MATILDA: You're not the only one who doesn't know how to do this, Gabe.

GABRIEL: I know. That's why I'm telling you this story. So, I freed the bird, well in as much as I got it out of the cat's mouth.

> *Beat.*

When an animal is completely overcome by a predator, no flight or fight left, it feigns death in a final attempt to make the predator stop attacking. I knew exactly what that bird was doing. Drinking is my version of playing dead.

> *Beat.*

I went to take the bird to the vet but … I woke up in what I think was the next day, with a dead bird, in my pocket. I—I was lying in my own shit with a dead bird in my pocket. My father would have been proud of me.

> *Beat.*

I must have sat at a pub drinking while a bird died in my pocket. Do you think that matters?

> *Pause.*

We could go to the pub, and take the question off the table? Because this stuff, these questions only make their way to the surface when I'm sober. I drink for a reason, you know. Come on, I will take you out for a drink and we can talk about the elephant in the room, a man in a hospital bed with a brain haemorrhage. Believe me, a few drinks and I will be able to do it, talk about it, in whatever way you want—

MATILDA: Gabriel—

GABRIEL: With tears, a smile, just put in your order and I will be able to do it if I have a drink. I'll be fine.

Beat.

How is he?

MATILDA: Not good. He is not going to be okay, Gabriel. His brain is damaged.

Silence.

Everyone has shame. Everyone, Gabriel. Everyone has some version of a dead bird in their pocket. This is rock bottom, it is time to stop digging, Gabriel.

Beat.

GABRIEL: I liked you better when you read Russian books—

MATILDA: I still read Russian—

GABRIEL: And tough love pamphlets—

MATILDA: Stop being a fucking coward! Sorry. Please, don't be a coward.

Beat.

Let me show you how it is done, you look the most painful thing you can think of square in the face. Look at me.

Beat.

Despite myself, I love you, but you don't love me, you will never love me. Even if you get sober, you will not love me. I am not an idiot. I am just no good at pain. Like you, no good at it, but I'm not a fucking coward, I can't afford to be because I am having a child.

Beat.

That's how it is done, Gabriel, so whatever it is, look it in the face because drinking won't make it go away.

GABRIEL: I'm sorry.

Beat. MATILDA *breaks off a piece of Toblerone and eats it calmly.*

MATILDA: So this is it, the beginning of never being the same.

She proceeds to break the Toblerone into pieces.

See, it's not that big. How is it, we learn to walk, talk, read, drive, ride a bike, put someone on the bloody moon, but we don't know how to fall out of love, or stop falling in love. Don't contact me until you're sober.

MATILDA *exits.*

SCENE TWELVE—BOUNCE

A park / Angela and Tony's flat. ANGELA *stands at the foot of the cat's grave.* GABRIEL *joins her. They both stand in silence for a while.* GABRIEL *refers to the stick cross at the head of the grave.*

GABRIEL: He wasn't religious.

ANGELA: You still giving cats human qualities?

GABRIEL: You're the one who put a crucifix at the end of his grave—

ANGELA: Tony wanted to put it there, brain damage and religion— Sorry, can't believe I said that. I'm tired.

GABRIEL: Are you alright?

ANGELA: Yes.

GABRIEL: Do you need help?

ANGELA: We really have done the full circle, do I need help?

GABRIEL: Do you?

ANGELA: No. Thank you.

> *She gets a present out of her bag and places it between* GABRIEL *and herself.*

Don't open it now, I don't want to be here when you open it.

GABRIEL: Okay— Shit!

ANGELA: What?

GABRIEL: Forgot the shovel.

ANGELA: That cat was an arsehole. Should have cremated him.

GABRIEL: I did tell you I was in no condition to be digging a hole that night.

ANGELA: You were in no condition for anything before you buried this little fucker.

GABRIEL: People love to hate him, look at my book—

ANGELA: How you going with that?

GABRIEL: 'This is a horrible book, about a horrible man, it makes you wonder whether Gabriel Freeman himself is a horrible man. One point five stars.'

ANGELA: I read it.

GABRIEL: Awful when the fuckers are right.

Beat.

I haven't been able to write since I got sober.

ANGELA: Give it time.

She touches his heart.

Go back in there. That's where your book is, Gabriel.

GABRIEL: I might have pickled it.

Beat.

I've had to start a data entry job.

ANGELA: Really?

GABRIEL: Yep, and here's the kicker. Matilda is my supervisor—

ANGELA *laughs.*

It's not funny.

ANGELA: It's a little funny.

GABRIEL: Step one—I admit that I am powerless over alcohol and powerless over Matilda.

ANGELA: How is Matilda?

GABRIEL: She got a dog. An Irish Wolfhound called Count Alexey Kirillovitch Vronsky. Lexi for short.

ANGELA: …?

GABRIEL: Character from *Anna Karenina*. And she has started seeing the owner of our local bookshop—

ANGELA *is laughing.*

Stop it. And she has enrolled in a Russian Literature course—*Stop!*

ANGELA: It is a little funny.

GABRIEL: Fucking hilarious!

ANGELA: Good on her.

GABRIEL: Yep, she never stops being brilliant. Mr Bookshop can't stop telling her he loves her, she can't stand it. And the more she bosses him round, the more he falls, it's fantastic.

Beat.

How is Tony?

ANGELA: He still can't do stairs and yesterday he introduced himself to one of the physios as 'The Cat Killer'. It is really, really—it is so hard, Gabriel. The last words he said to me before he collapsed were 'Don't come near me'. Now he can't let go of me, needs me for everything.

GABRIEL: Does he know you're seeing me today?

ANGELA: He doesn't remember who you are. There's no figuring it. What the brain holds on to. He still hates cats but you're off the hook. I envy him sometimes.

GABRIEL: No you don't.

Pause.

Can I show you a photo, Ange?

ANGELA: Yes.

GABRIEL *shows her a photo of his son.*

GABRIEL: Six months.

ANGELA: He is you all over.

GABRIEL: Terrifying.

ANGELA: He's beautiful.

Beat.

What do you want, Gabe?

GABRIEL: Thank you for meeting me.

ANGELA: What do you want?

GABRIEL: I left the hardest till last—

ANGELA: Don't—

GABRIEL: I'm sorry.

ANGELA: Yep.

Pause.

GABRIEL: He just reached out with his tiny hand one day, wanting this plastic container I was holding, and when I handed it to him, the joy on his face. It broke me. I've been sober for five months. And I know you've heard it one hundred times. And I am not saying every day is not a new proposition and a challenge, and that I don't have to call— beg a higher power—I do, but it is different. I'm different.

ANGELA: No. We will always know what we did to each other. You drank, and I chose to humiliate myself by tolerating it. That will always be what happened. We can't change it. We're done. You know this, Gabe.

GABRIEL: It's different, I swear, we're different—

ANGELA: We're not different, Gabriel! People lose in love all the time. We lost. This is us, Gabriel. You go first.

GABRIEL: What?

ANGELA: Say goodbye.

GABRIEL: You broke my heart—

ANGELA: No, I asked you to stop drinking, Gabriel. And you've stopped, and don't get me wrong, I have nothing but goodwill towards your sobriety, I really do, but my heart has been beating backwards since the day I met you. I am asking you to say goodbye to me. Seven years, Gabe, say goodbye, it is the least you could do if you really do love me.

> *Beat.*

Let go.

> *She removes her hand from his.*

Promise me you will go to a meeting today.

GABRIEL: I promise.

ANGELA: Promise yourself. Every day. Every single day.

SCENE THIRTEEN—LOVE

GABRIEL *opens the present from* ANGELA.

TONY *is seated and* ANGELA *is at his feet.* ANGELA *taps* TONY*'s right leg.* TONY *lifts his foot.*

Note—these two scenes take place simultaneously.

ANGELA: Right foot.

> TONY *lifts his right foot and* ANGELA *puts a sock and sandshoe on it.*

Left foot.

> TONY *lifts his left foot and* ANGELA *puts a sock and shoe on the foot.*

TONY: Which one are you?

ANGELA: Angela.

The job is done, but fatigue sees ANGELA *stay on her knees for a little longer.* GABRIEL *holds up the present, a size one baby's jumpsuit.*

TONY: What now?

ANGELA: Stand up.

TONY: Now?

ANGELA: Now. You can do this.

She gets to her feet to support TONY.

We can do this. Come on.

ANGELA *helps* TONY *stand.* GABRIEL *stands at the same time. He looks at* ANGELA. *He watches her throughout the scene.*

TONY: Which one are you?

ANGELA: I'm Angela.

TONY: You look funny.

ANGELA: I am funny. You know me.

TONY: I know you. Funny face. And you know me.

ANGELA: That's right.

TONY: Angela.

ANGELA: That's right.

TONY: Sad funny face.

ANGELA: That's me.

TONY: Are you the one I love?

ANGELA: Yes.

TONY: What now?

ANGELA: We walk.

TONY: Don't leave me—

ANGELA: I'm not leaving you.

TONY: Don't walk away from me.

ANGELA: I'm not. You can do this.

TONY *walks with* ANGELA.

Now hold on to the windowsill.

TONY: Don't let me go.

ANGELA *removes* TONY*'s hands from hers and places them on the windowsill.*

What's happening?
ANGELA: You know this.
TONY: No?
ANGELA: We practise.
TONY: And you do it with me.
ANGELA: Yes.

Pause.

TONY: What now?
ANGELA: We keep practising.
TONY: Which one?
ANGELA: You know which one.
TONY: Standing alone?
ANGELA: Standing alone.

GABRIEL *stands and* TONY *slowly lifts his hands off the windowsill.*

TONY: What now?
ANGELA: We walk again.
TONY: Where?
ANGELA: Towards me.
TONY: Towards you.
ANGELA: One step at a time. Towards the one you love.

THE END

RIFFIN THEATRE COMPANY PRESENTS

DEAD CAT BOUNCE

Y MARY RACHEL BROWN

BW STABLES THEATRE
FEBRUARY – 6 APRIL 2019

RECTOR
TCHELL BUTEL
SIGNER
NEVIEVE BLANCHETT
HTING DESIGNER
EXANDER BERLAGE
MPOSER & SOUND DESIGNER
TE EDMONDSON
AGE MANAGER
CHELLE SVERDLOFF
AGE MANAGEMENT
CONDMENT
NNIFER JACKSON

TH
TE CHEEL
CIA MASTRANTONE
HNNY NASSER
SH QUONG TART

GRIFFIN
THEATRE
COMPANY

Australian Government | Australia Council for the Arts

n acknowledges the generosity of the
orn, Broughton & Walford Foundation in
ing it the use of the SBW Stables Theatre
ree, less outgoings, since 1986.

PLAYWRIGHT'S NOTE

Dead Cat Bounce is about the ripple effect of addiction, and the toll it takes on one's ability to give and receive love. All the characters in this play are addicted to something or someone. At its heart, this is a story of unrequited love, a predicament that brings out the best and worst of human behaviour. Unfolding my characters' survival techniques in the face of heartbreak was a challenge, and I relished it. Losing in love can create unseen heroic acts of restraint and sacrifice. The reserves people find in the face of heartbreak is of great interest to me as a playwright and a human being, who, like everyone, harbours secret struggles.

I consider it my job to rip the band-aid off what we find hard to say and do in life. In their own particular way, all the characters in *Dead Cat Bounce* carry shame and their forward movement is dependent on the admission of that shame. I hope their journeys make people feel a little less alone when they leave the theatre.

I had some wonderful journey-women and -men on this project. The Lysicrates Foundation commissioned this work, the playwriting community and I are indebted to their mission in the support of new Australian writing. Hilary Bell and Mitchell Butel supported me with some wise dramaturgical advice. I am grateful for their intelligence and care.

It is a thrill to have my work birthed on the Griffin stage, it is such a charged and live space. I also feel very blessed to have my words in the hands of such great actors and talented creatives.

Last but not least, dear Neil, thank you for sharing so much and encouraging me to be brave and put more of myself into my work. I did open heart surgery on this one because of your simple and true words.

Mary Rachel Brown
Writer

DIRECTOR'S
NOTE

The heart wants what it wants... So said American poet Emily Dickinson and those words ring true for Mary Rachel Brown's extraordinarily tender, tough and insightful play. Like an Antipodean Chekhov, she writes characters who want what they shouldn't want, want what they perhaps can't have, want back what they once held. Or indeed, those who want to break free of the addictions and needs that lie within them. It has been an utter joy, education and privilege to work on this great play with Mary and with such a fine, talented and generous cast, creative team and crew. My thanks to all of them and to other artists who have worked on earlier incarnations of this play—Richard Sydenham, Lena Cruz, Linda Cropper and John Gaden. Thanks too to Lee Lewis and the Griffin team for their faith in me and for ensuring great works such as Mary's play are given such a wonderful platform in this little jewel of a theatre.

Mitchell Butel
Director

MARY RACHEL BROWN
PLAYWRIGHT

Mary Rachel Brown is a playwright and dramaturg based in Sydney. Mary's playwriting credits include: for Griffin Independent/Apocalypse Theatre Company/Glen Street Theatre/HotHouse/Merrigong Theatre Company: *The Dapto Chaser*; for Apocalypse Theatre Company/Old 505: *All My Sleep And Waking*; for Apocalypse Theatre Company/Red Line Productions: *Permission to Spin*; for the Australian War Memorial: *Last Letters*; for Christine Dunstan Productions: *Inside Out*; for Darlinghurst Theatre Company: *Silent Night*; for Glynn Nicholas Group: *National Security and the Art of Taxidermy*; for South East Arts: *Sunshine*; for Sydney Conservatorium of Music: *Die Fledermaus* (adaptation); and for the University of Wollongong: *These Are Not My People*. Mary's TV credits include: for the ABC: *The Elegant Gentleman's Guide to Knife Fighting*; and for Seven Network: *Home and Away*. Mary is the recipient of several national playwriting awards, including Griffin's Lysicrates Prize in 2016, the 2006 Griffin Award, PWA's Max Afford Award in 2007 and SBW Foundation's Rodney Seaborn Award in 2008. Mary has worked as a dramaturg for PWA, Canberra Theatre Centre, ATYP, Canberra Youth Theatre and the Australian War Memorial. Mary is a proud member of the Australian Writers' Guild and supporter of WITS (Women in Theatre and Screen).

MITCHELL BUTEL
DIRECTOR

Mitchell holds four Helpmann Awards, three Sydney Theatre Awards and two Green Room Awards for his work in Australian theatre over the past two decades as both a performer and a director. He also holds two AFI nominations for his work in Australian feature films. As a director, Mitchell's theatre credits include: for Griffin Theatre Company's Lysicrates Prize: *Approximate Balance*; for ATYP: *Spring Awakening,* which won the Sydney Theatre Award's Best Production for Young People; for Blue Saint/ Hayes Theatre: *Violet*, which received three Sydney Theatre Awards, including Best Director of a Musical and Best Production of an Independent Musical; for Ensemble Theatre: *Marjorie Prime*; for Sydney Philharmonia Choirs: *Candide*; for Sydney Symphony Orchestra: *Funny Girl*, *Porgy and Bess, The Bernstein Songbook;* and as Co-Director: for Darlinghurst Theatre Company: *An Act of God*. Mitchell wrote and directed *Killing Time* for Adelaide Cabaret Festival/Brisbane Cabaret Festival/SummerSalt Festival, and has written material for the Belvoir/Malthouse Theatre co-production of *The Government Inspector*, Opera Australia's *The Mikado*, and the Sydney Festival/Malthouse Theatre co-production of Meow Meow's *Little Match Girl*. He has also performed for Griffin in *Emerald City*. Mitchell was recently appointed Artistic Director of the State Theatre Company of South Australia. He is a proud member of Actors Equity.

GENEVIEVE BLANCHETT
DESIGNER

Genevieve is a multi-disciplinary designer. She holds a Bachelor of Design in Theatre (NIDA), a Bachelor of Design in Architecture (USYD) and a Masters of Urban Design and Development (UNSW). Genevieve has designed sets and costumes for many of Australia's leading theatre companies, including: for Griffin Theatre Company *(The Modern International Dead, Wolf Lullaby)*, Bell Shakespeare, Belvoir, Melbourne Theatre Company, Queensland Theatre, State Theatre Company of South Australia, Sydney Chamber Opera, Sydney Festival and Sydney Theatre Company. Internationally, Genevieve has designed productions for the Druid Theatre, Edinburgh Festival, New Zealand Opera and Seattle Opera. Recent project credits include: public space event/activation designs for BIG hART and the City of Sydney: *Walk to Memel* (Barangaroo); site design and logistics for the CORRIDOR Project: *Big Little Histories of Canowindra*; developing an operating framework and concept design for an experimental augmented reality app featuring opera with Google and OQ; and advising on cultural strategy for projects with the City of Parramatta. Genevieve was a founding board member of Emergency Architects Australia, founded the Sydney chapter of Architecture for Humanity and, with Jennifer van den Bussche, co-founded Sticky Situations—an award-winning arts-based community development not-for-profit in Johannesburg. Genevieve currently sits on the Parramatta Riverside Theatres Advisory Board, the Parramatta Female Factory Precinct Association Board and is a member of the Urban Growth Stakeholder Collaboration forum for The Precinct.

ALEXANDER BERLAGE
LIGHTING DESIGNER

Alexander Berlage is a Sydney-based lighting designer and director. His lighting design credits include: for Griffin: *Good Cook. Friendly. Clean.*; for Griffin Independent: *Nosferatutu or Bleeding at the Ballet, Thomas Murray and the Upside Down River*; for 25A/Belvoir: *The Overcoat*; for ATYP: *Between Us, Luke Lloyd: Alienoid, Moth, War Crimes*; for Critical Stages: *4000 Miles, Songs for the Fallen, Stones in his Pockets*; for Ensemble Theatre: *Buyer and Cellar, The Kitchen Sink, Marjorie Prime, Unqualified*; for Hayes Theatre Co.: *Cry-Baby, Dogfight, Everybody Loves Lucy, High Fidelity*; for Old 505 Theatre: *The Block Universe, Hilt, Home Invasion*; for Red Line Productions at the Old Fitz Theatre: *4:48 Psychosis*, for which he won the 2017 Sydney Theatre Award for Best Lighting Designer for an Independent Production, *The Bitter Tears of Petra Von Kant* (Sydney Theatre Award nomination), *Crimes of the Heart, Doubt* (Sydney Theatre Award nomination), *The Effect, Freak Winds, Howie the Rookie, The Judas Kiss, Men, there will be a climax, Vertical Dreaming, The Whale* (Sydney Theatre Award nomination); for Sydney Chamber Opera: *An Index of Metals* (Associate), *La Passion de Simone, Resonant Bodies, Victory Over the Sun*; for Sydney Dance Company: *New Breed 2018, PPY15*:

Revealed, PPY18: Revealed; for Sydney Theatre Company: Cloud Nine, Lethal Indifference. Alexander was visual director on Resonant Bodies for Sydney Chamber Opera. His director credits include: for An Assorted Few: The Van De Maar Papers; for Hayes Theatre Co. and LPD Productions: Cry-Baby (nine Sydney Theatre Award nominations including Best Director of a Musical and Best Production of a Musical); for Old 505 Theatre and An Assorted Few: Home Invasion (Sydney Theatre Award nomination); for Red Line Productions at the Old Fitz Theatre and An Assorted Few: there will be a climax (Sydney Theatre Award nominations for Best Independent Production and Best Direction of an Independent Production).

NATE EDMONDSON
COMPOSER & SOUND DESIGNER

Nate is an international, multi-award winning composer and sound designer for stage and screen. His theatre credits include: for Griffin: Caress/Ache, Good Cook. Friendly. Clean., Jump for Jordan, This Year's Ashes, The Witches; for Griffin Independent: The Ham Funeral, Rust and Bone, MinusOneSister, Music; for ATYP: Fireface, The Hiding Place, Political Children; for Bell Shakespeare: A Midsummer Night's Dream, Julius Caesar, Macbeth, Romeo and Juliet, The Tempest, The Winter's Tale; for Belvoir: Mark Colvin's Kidney, Mortido, Seventeen, This Heaven; for Critical Stages: Stones in his Pockets; for Darlinghurst Theatre Company: All My Sons, Daylight Saving, Good Works, Love, Savages, The Seafarer, The Paris Letter, Torch Song Trilogy; for Ensemble Theatre: Baby Doll, Diplomacy; for KXT/ bAKEHOUSE: Jatinga, Leaves, for which Nate won the 2016 Broadway World Award for Best Score/ Sound Design of a Play, Straight; for Little Ones Theatre: Psycho Beach Party, Salomé, Two by Two; for Malthouse Theatre: Lord of the Flies, Salomé; for New Theatre: Marat/Sade, When The Rain Stops Falling; for Red Line Productions: Bengal Tiger at the Baghdad Zoo, I Am My Own Wife, The Village Bike; for Riverside Theatres: Shellshock; for Rockefeller Productions: That Golden Girls Show! (US), The Very Hungry Caterpillar Show (AU, NZ, US, UAE & UK); for Seymour Centre: Blackrock, The Flick; for Siren Theatre Company: Good With Maps (AU & UK), Misterman (AU & UK), for both of which Nate won the Sydney Theatre Award for Best Score/Sound Design of an Independent Production, The Moors, The Trouble With Harry (AU & UK); for Sport For Jove: Of Mice and Men; for Street Theatre: All My Sons (UK), for which Nate won the 2014 Brian Dyer Trophy for Best Score/Sound Design; for Sydney Dance Company: Once We Were; for Sydney Theatre Company: A Midsummer Night's Dream, Blackie Blackie Brown, Cloud Nine, The Harp in the South Parts I and II, Never Did Me Any Harm (with Force Majeure), Romeo and Juliet, Three Sisters.

MICHELLE SVERDLOFF
STAGE MANAGER

Michelle is a theatre-maker, producer and stage manager. Her stage management credits include: for Griffin: *The Almighty Sometimes*; for Bell Shakespeare: *The Players* (in-school performances); for Bontom Entertainment: *Chamber Pot Opera*; for CDP Theatre Producers: *The Very Hungry Caterpillar Show* (Australian Tour); for Erth Visual & Physical Inc. for Vivid Festival: *The Liminal Hour*; for Heartbeat Opera NYC: Heartbeat Opera Festival; for Jack Arts NYC: *The Geneva Project*; for Northern Rivers Performing Arts: *Railway Wonderland*; for Punchdrunk Theatre Company: *Sleep No More*. Michelle has also completed professional secondments at Casula Powerhouse Arts Centre, Mullum Circus Festival and Belvoir. She graduated with a Bachelor of Communication (Theatre/Media) from Charles Sturt University in 2014.

KATE CHEEL
MATILDA

Kate has worked consistently on stage and screen since graduating from Adelaide College of the Arts. Theatre credits include: for Griffin/State Theatre Company of South Australia: *Masquerade;* for Griffin Independent/Stories Like These: *MinusOneSister*; for 25A/Belvoir: *The Overcoat*; for An Assorted Few: *Home Invasion*; for ATYP: *Spring Awakening,* for which she was nominated for the Sydney Theatre Award for Best Supporting Actress in a Musical; for Outhouse Theatre Company: *4 Minutes 12 Seconds*; for State Theatre Company of South Australia: *Hedda Gabler, The Glass Menagerie, Jesikah, That Eye, The Sky, Three Sisters*; for Windmill Theatre Company: *Big Bad Wolf, Fugitive*; and internationally: for Kneehigh Theatre (UK): *Brief Encounter.* In 2018, she played the lead role in the AACTA-nominated feature film *Strange Colours*, which had its premiere at the Venice Film Festival. Other film credits include *One Eyed Girl*; and her television credits include: for the ABC: *Riot, The Letdown.* Kate was awarded the Emerging Artist of the Year by the Adelaide Critics Circle, was a recipient of the Adele Koh Scholarship, and was a recipient of the Neil Curnow Award.

LUCIA MASTRANTONE
ANGELA

Lucia has performed in Griffin's *Kill Climate Deniers* and *Ladies Day*. Some of her other theatre credits include: for Belvoir: *Atlantis*, *The Book of Everything*, *Love and Magic in Mama's Kitchen*, *Macbeth*, *Popular Mechanicals 1 & 2*, *Scorched*, *Twelfth Night*, *Vicious Angel*; for Bell Shakespeare: *The Duchess of Malfi*; for Darlinghurst Theatre Company: *The Hypochondriac*; for Melbourne Theatre Company: *Venetian Twins*; for State Theatre Company of South Australia: *A Little Like Drowning*, *The Merchant of Venice*, *The Rover*, *Six Characters in Search of an Author*; for Sydney Theatre Company: *The Harp in the South Parts I and II*, *Mariage Blanc*, *Romeo and Juliet*, *Talk*. Lucia's physical theatre credits include: for Legs on the Wall: *Under the Influence*; for Magpie Theatre/Melbourne Theatre Company: *Little Miss Hood*, *Verona*; for Not Yet It's Difficult: *Running Show*; for Shaun Parker Co: *Blue Love*; for Urban Theatre Projects: *The Longest Night*. Lucia worked as the Associate Director/Movement Director for *The Baulkham Hills African Ladies Troupe* at Belvoir/Sydney Opera House. Lucia's screen appearances include acclaimed TV series *Tangle*, ABC TV's *Rake* and AFI Award-winning films *Bad Boy Bubby* and *Look Both Ways*. Lucia is currently co-starring in a new animation comedy series produced by Working Dog called *Pacific Heat*.

JOHNNY NASSER
TONY

Johnny Nasser is a National Theatre Drama School graduate and has worked across various theatre, TV and film projects over the last 15 years. He has created and devised theatre seen throughout Australia, Asia and the Middle East. Johnny's theatre credits include: for Griffin Independent/Siren Theatre Company: *The Ham Funeral*, for which Johnny won the Sydney Theatre Award for Best Supporting Actor; for Belvoir/Riverside Theatres: *Wilde Tales*; for CDP: *52 Storey Treehouse*, *Mr Stink*; for KXT: *Night Slows Down*; for NIDA: *Arabian Night*; for NORPA: *Railway Wonderland*; for Red Line Productions at the Old Fitz Theatre: *The Effect*; for Riverside: *All the Blood & All the Water*; for Sydney Opera House: *Darlingwood Tales*, *Monkeyshines*; for UAE: *Clusters of Light*. TV credits include: for ABC: *Chandon Pictures*; for Network Ten: *Legacy of the Silver Shadow*, *Street Smart*; for Nine Network: *Here Come the Habibs*, *Stingers*; for Seven Network: *Home and Away*. Feature film credits include: *Convict*, *The Combination*, and the upcoming *The Combination: Redemption*.

JOSH QUONG TART
GABE

Josh recently appeared as Ron Austin in the award-winning ABC telemovie *Riot*. His extensive television credits also include: for the ABC: *Fancy Boy, Rake, The Elegant Gentleman's Guide to Knife-Fighting;* for FX: *Mr Inbetween*; for Nine Network: *Hyde and Seek, The Great Mint Swindle, Underbelly: Badness*; for Seven Network: *All Saints; Home and Away*; and internationally: for USA Network: *The Starter Wife*. Josh's feature film credits include *Around the Block, Down Under*, and *Scare Campaign*. He will also appear in Abe Forsythe's forthcoming horror-comedy *Little Monsters*. Josh's theatre credits include: for Bell Shakespeare: *Romeo and Juliet;* for B Sharp: *Killer Joe;* for The Directory: *La Dispute, The Mirage*; for Ensemble Theatre: *This Lime Tree Bower;* for Red Line Productions at the Old Fitz: *The Judas Kiss*; for Sydney Theatre Company: *Mother Courage and Her Children, The Miser, Our Town, Troopers, Wharf Revue: Red Wharf;* and for Tamarama Rock Surfers: *Rope*. Josh was nominated for the Helpmann Award for Best Actor in a Musical for Disney's *The Lion King*, playing the villain Scar. He graduated from NIDA in 1997.

ABOUT GRIFFIN

"If you've ever sat in the theatre and thought, 'those actors are just too damn far away', then Griffin is for you."
– Concrete Playground

Located in the heart of Kings Cross— in the historic SBW Stables Theatre— Griffin has been dedicated to bringing the best Australian stories to the stage for the better part of four decades.

We're passionate about theatre that's written by Australians, about Australians, for Australians to enjoy. Iconic Aussie plays such as *The Boys, Holding the Man, The Heartbreak Kid* and *The Bleeding Tree* all had their world premieres at Griffin. And many of our nation's most celebrated artists started their professional careers with us— Cate Blanchett, David Wenham, Michael Gow and Louis Nowra to name a few.

*Homegrown inspiration
By you, for you.*

GRIFFIN THEATRE COMPANY
13 Craigend St
Kings Cross NSW 2011

02 9332 1052
info@griffintheatre.com.au
griffintheatre.com.au

SBW STABLES THEATRE
10 Nimrod St
Kings Cross NSW 2011

BOOKINGS
griffintheatre.com.au
02 9361 3817

GRIFFIN FAMILY

[handwritten notes:] KOM PAPER TO PLAY → PERFORMANCE PEOPLE

GRIFFIN DONORS

Income from Griffin activities covers less than 40% of our operating costs—leaving an ever increasing gap for us to fill through government funding, sponsorship and the generosity of o individual supporters. Your support helps us bridge the gap and keep ticket prices affordable and our work at its best. To make a donation and a difference, contact Griffin on **9332 1052** o donate online at **griffintheatre.com.au**

FOUNDATIONS
Production Partner
Girgensohn Foundation

Robertson Foundation
CAL Cultural Fund
Malcolm Robertson Foundation
Darin Cooper Foundation

Creative Partnerships Australia
through the Plus1 Program

STUDIO PROGRAM
Gil Appleton
Darin Cooper Foundation
Limb Family Foundation
Malcolm Robertson Foundation
Peter Graves
Ken & Lilian Horler
Rhonda McIver
Pip Rath & Wayne Lonergan
Geoff & Wendy Simpson
Danielle Smith
Walking up the Hill Foundation

PRODUCTION PARTNERS 2019
Prima Facie
Production Patrons
Robert Dick & Erin Shiel
Richard McHugh & Kate Morgan

Production Supporters
Richard Weinstein &
Richard Benedict

City of Gold
Production Patrons
Ann & Brian O'Connell (in memoriam)
Malcolm Robertson Foundation
The Sky Foundation

Production Supporters
David Marr & Sebastian
Tesoriero

SEASON DONORS
Front Row Donors +$10,000
Darin Cooper Foundation
Robert Dick & Erin Shiel
Ingrid Kaiser
Anthony & Suzanne
Maple-Brown
Rebel Penfold-Russell
Pip Rath & Wayne Lonergan

Main Stage Donor
$5,000 - $9,999
Anonymous (1)
Louise Christie
Lyndell & Daniel Droga
Peter Graves
Helen & Abraham James &
Family
Lee Lewis & Brett Boardman
Sophie McCarthy & Antony Green
Bruce Meagher & Greg Waters
Peter & Dianne O'Connell
Don & Leslie Parsonage
Sue Procter
The Robertson Foundation
Geoff & Wendy Simpson
The Sky Foundation
Merilyn Sleigh &
Raoul de Ferranti

Final Draft
$2,000-$4,999
Gae Anderson
Baly Douglass Foundation
Lisa Barker and
Don Russell
Helen Bauer & Helen Lynch AM
Ellen Borda
Marilyn & David Boyer
Bernard Coles
Alan Colletti
Bryony & Tim Cox
Lachlan Edwards
Elizabeth Fullerton
Kathy Glass
Libby Higgin
Ro & John Knox
Kiong Lee & Richard Funston
David Marr & Sebastian
Tesoriero
Carina G. Martin
John Mitchell
David Nguyen
Anthony Paull
Julia Pincus
Chris Reed
Tea Uglow
Richard Weinstein & Richard Benedict

Workshop Donor
$1,000-$1,999
Anonymous (3)
Brian Abel
Antoinette Albert
Michael & Charmaine Bra
Jane Bridge
Corinne & Bryan
Iolanda Capodanno
Elaine Chia and
Ettore Altomare
Sally Crawford
Nathan Croft & James Wh
Cris Croker and David Wes
Carol Dettmann
Christine Dunstan
Ros & Paul Espie
Rowena Falzon
John & Libby Fairfax
Peter Gray & Helen Thwai
Judge Joe Harman
James Hartwright &
Kerrin D'Arcy
John Head
Mary Holt
Peter Ingle
Margaret Johnston
David & Adrienne Kitching
Jennifer Ledgar & Bob Lin
Richard & Elizabeth Long
John McCallum
Elaine & Bill McLaughlin
Dr Steve McNamara
Kent and Sandra McPhee
Dr Wendy Michaels
Joy Minter
Catriona Morgan-Hunn
Tommy Murphy
Ian Neuss
Martin Portus
Steve & Belinda Rankine
Steve Riethoff
Annabel Ritchie
Sylvia Rosenblum
Geoffrey Starr
Robyn Stone
Adam Suckling & Pip McGuinness
Augusta Supple
Peter Talbot
Stuart Thomas

GRIFFIN DONORS

Mike Thompson
Daniel P. Tobin
Janet Wahlquist
David West
Paul & Jennifer Winch
Simone Whetton
Elizabeth Wing

Reading Donor
$500-$999

Anonymous (1)
Susan Ambler
Jes Andersen
Wendy Ashton
Robyn Ayres
Melissa Ball
Nikki Barrett
Karen Bedford
Penny Beran
Cherry & Peter Best
Tanja Boric
Jo Bradley
Simon Burke
Alex Byrne & Sue Hearn
Peter Chapman
Louise Diamond
Michael Diamond
Max Dingle
Tim Duggan
Wendy Elder
Bob Ernst
Brian Everingham
Robyn Fortescue &
Rosie Wagstaff
Jennifer Giles
Reg Graycar
Tonkin Zulaikha Greer
Anthony Gregg
Edwina Guinness
Con & Antonia Haralambis
Stephanie & Andrew Harrison
Mark Hopkinson and
Michelle Opie
David Hoskins & Paul
McKnight
Susan Hyde
Anne Loveridge
Ian & Elizabeth MacDonald
Chris Marrable
Christopher McCabe
Nicole Mckenna
Patrick McIntyre
Neville Mitchell
Jane Munro
Patricia Novikoff
Kerry O'Kane

Alex Oonagh Redmond
Carolyn Penfold
Ian Phipps
Roslyn Renwick
Karen Rodgers & Bill Harris
Gemma Rygate
Julianne Schultz
Diana Simmonds
Jann Skinner
Rob & Rae Spence
Ross Steele AM
Leslie Stern
Mary Stollery & Eric Dole
Andrew & Camilla Strang
Catherine Sullivan &
Alexandra Bowen
Sue Thomson
Ariadne Vromen
John Waters
Rosemary White

First Draft Donor
$200-$499

Anonymous (12)
Edwina Birch
Shay Bristowe
Wendy Buswell
G Carrick
Charlie Chan & Angela
Catterns
Amanda J. Clark
Sue Clark
Kate Collier
Carolyn Crawford
Bryan Cutler
Owen Davies
Marie Delaney
Susan Donnelly
Dr June Donsworth
Elizabeth Evatt
Paul Fletcher
Matt Garrett
Bryant George
Sarah & Braith Gilchrist
Brenda Gottsche
Priscilla Guest
Sue Hackett
Elizabeth Hanley
Belinda Hazelton
Janet Heffernan
Danielle Hoareau
Trish Howes
Sylvia Hrovatin
Matthew Huxtable
Marian & Nabeel Ibrahim
Diana Jefferson

C John Keightley
Ryan Kucharski
Penelope Latey
Gary Lawrence
Peta Leemen
Antoinette Le Marchant
Dr Peter Louw
Carolyn Lowry
Anni MacDougall
Michael Markiewicz
Robert Marks
Suz Mawer
Meg McDonald
Edward McGuiness
Duncan McKay
Ian McMillan
Sarah Miller
Bruce Milthorpe
Kate Mulvany
Margaret Murphy
Dian Neligan
Carolyn Newman
Jamie Oxenbould
Annie Page & Colin Fletcher
Meredith Phelps
Belinda Piggot & David
Ojerholm
Christopher Powell
Virginia Pursell
Francis W. Robertson
Ann Rocca
Catherine Rothery
David & Dianne Russell
Anne Schofield
Julia Selby
Vanda and Martin Smith
Stephen Thompson
Fiona Tinkler
Trisha Treanor
David Walsh
Katrina Weir
Cathy Wilcox
Eve Wynhausen
Aviva Ziegler

We would also like to thank
Peter O'Connell for his
expertise, guidance and time.

Current as of 7 February, 2019.

THANK You!!

SPONSORS

Government Supporters

Australian Government | Australia Council for the Arts

Create NSW
Arts, Screen & Culture

CREATIVE CITY SYDNEY

Patron

2018 Season Sponsor

alphabet.

Production Partner

GIRGENSOHN FOUNDATION

Major Partner

nabprivate
nab

Griffin Studio & Griffin Award

COPYRIGHT AGENCY
CULTURAL FUND

Griffin Studio

MALCOLM ROBERTSON FOUNDATION

Griffin Ambassadors & Artistic Associate Sponsor

ROBERTSON FOUNDATION

Company Lawyers

MARQUE

Brett Boardman Photography

Associate Sponsors

DeRepublica

Company Sponsors

íve

TimeOut

SATURDAY PAPER

THE UNIVERSITY OF SYDNEY
PERFORMANCE STUDIES

Rosenfeld, Kant & Co.
Business & Financial Solutions

MOFFITT

CURRENCY PRESS

Coopers

FOUR PILLARS

bourke street bakery

Access Partners

WeirAnderson FOUNDATION

DESIGNKINGCOMPANY

www.ingramcontent.com/pod-product-compliance
Lightning Source LLC
Chambersburg PA
CBHW050022090426
42734CB00021B/3380